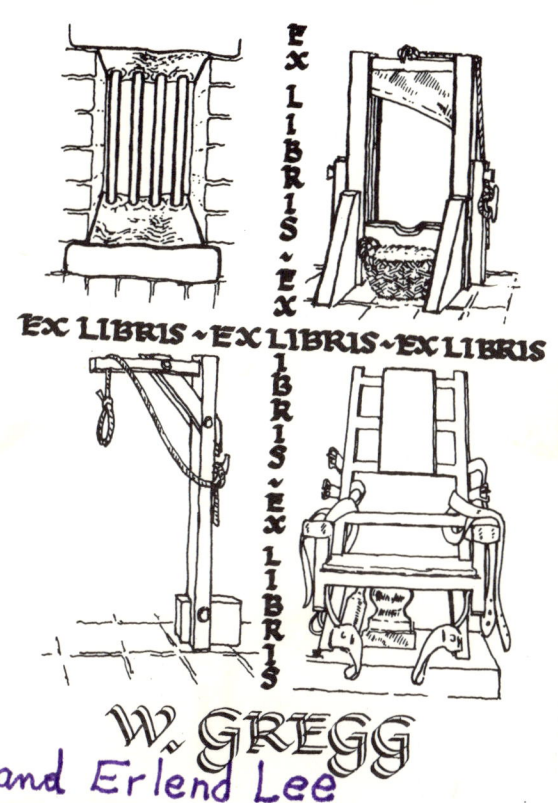

W. GREGG
and Erlend Lee

Tightrope

Tightrope

A Matter of Life and Death

The Autobiography of
Anna Reynolds

SIDGWICK & JACKSON
LONDON

This book is for Chrissie,
who is the bravest and the best,
and who deserves much more
than a book dedication

First published in Great Britain in 1990 by Sidgwick & Jackson Limited

Copyright © Anna Reynolds 1991

All rights reserved. No part of this book may be reproduced or transmitted in any form or by any means, electronic or mechanical, including photocopying, recording or by any information storage and retrieval system, without permission in writing from the Publisher.

ISBN 0-283-99867 9

Typeset by Matrix, Covent Garden, London WC2B 5HP

Printed by Mackays of Chatham PLC, Chatham, Kent
for Sidgwick & Jackson Limited
1 Tavistock Chambers, Bloomsbury Way
London WC1A S2G

Contents

Acknowledgements vii

Prologue ix

Chapter 1   1
Chapter 2   5
Chapter 3   27
Chapter 4   54
Chapter 5   74
Chapter 6   91
Chapter 7   109
Chapter 8   121
Chapter 9   142
Chapter 10   153
Chapter 11   159
Chapter 12   175

Epilogue 195

Acknowledgements

There are so many, many people whom I could list here, and will: thanks to Pam, for everything; to Ken and Jo, for being there; to Debb, Paul, Chris, Cyril and Davey, for their contribution; to Maggie and Linda, who are pearls beyond price; to Graham, for being a caring professional; to Andy W., for sharing some of the pain; to Dr Dalton, in her ceaseless campaign; to Roy, for putting up with me; to Judith and Jonathan and all the campaigners who fought so hard and so successfully; to Jude, for gritting her teeth and talking me through the bad times; to Donna and all her sisters who, despite their own agony, gave strength to me; to Sister Austin, for her tireless work in prison and her ever-present sense of hope and light; to all the people I met along the way who gave me some of themselves; to Henry and the other two, for comfort and love; to all my friends who have put up with me during the writing of this book; to Susan, for her perceptive and intuitive editing; to Lucinda, for believing in it; and, finally, to the man I love, who has selflessly steered me through the worst and gone hand in hand with me until we reached the best.

Prologue

The day of the final stage of the hearing was sunny, although I hardly noticed it. It did not matter to me. There were no clouds at all in the sky, and those with me removed their thick serge jackets and mopped their red, sweaty faces. They turned to me, curious and ready to be sympathetic. I replied in monosyllabic monotone to their polite small talk.

We were there in minutes – no hold-ups or wrong addresses this time. The building seemed as intimidating and tall as ever. I shivered and looked up, up, up at the point where stone gave way to sky. Last out of the vehicle, I answered the usual questions, futile, asked by the woman with me and climbed out, shaky-legged suddenly, sweat cold on my skin that was so unused to outside air.

The others stood around me in little groups, casting occasional anxious looks at me. I seemed to be seeing them as if through glass, smeared and misty. I felt sick. They began to move towards me and I swayed a little, not wanting to make a scene. It was too late to go back now. I had set the wheels of my fate in motion and once more they had brought me full circle, in the month, although two years on, of Alex's birth, in spring, the season of new birth and hope, the time of renewal. And I walked forward.

Chapter One

On the Friday, Friday the 13th, the judge briefly summed up, a neutral, pompous, long-winded speech that made some jurors' eyes glaze over. The jury went out at about ten o'clock. I was bailed on that last day, oddly, to stay within the confines of the court. Every day previously I had been sent down into the cells to await the court's return. Now, on the last possible day, the worst, the most tense, I was allowed some comparative freedom. I trailed miserably out to the ante-room behind the actual court room and perched on the edge of a table. It could be a long wait. The nurse and the two probation officers with me tried valiantly to keep me out of trouble, like you might amuse a small child. They brought me coffee, sweets, magazines, papers. They tried to interest me in the fashion pages and the crossword and discussed the weather, the weekend's prospects, sport. I sat silently irritated by their chatter, which was mostly for my benefit. At one point the judge passed through the ante-room on his way somewhere, followed by a scurrying clerk. This image of ceremonial made an uneasy bedfellow with the informality of the room where I and the detectives lounged, restless. Smoke filled the air. The judge looked carefully at me, possibly trying to remember who I was.

The time passed unbearably slowly in a vat of tedium. I knew what was going to happen, and now this – the wait for a verdict, the sentencing – was all a formality. I longed for the safety and inevitable chaos of women-only space in Holloway. At that moment, anything was better than the loneliness and fear of the hospital.

The jury came back at about eleven o'clock, needing more instructions. Then out we all trooped once again. I felt immeasurably tired already. The clock ticked too loudly, and I knew a moment's insane inappropriate irritation with the ugly plastic face. The jurors came back twice more before one o'clock, then the judge announced that the court would resume after lunch.

After lunch – non-existent for me, stomach churning in a sickly way already – the jury were hardly back out before they returned to ask if the judge would accept a majority verdict of 10–2 or less. He grunted his assent and out they went. Everyone was clock-watching now, conscious of their weekend slipping away from them.

At about 4.30 they were back with a final query; the judge, exasperated by now, told them that they would simply have to bring in a verdict within the next thirty minutes, because he was going away for the weekend and then starting a new case on the Monday, so the trial could not possibly be extended. With this time limit and veiled threat they were sent out again.

Within the half-hour they were back, finality upon their averted faces, and I knew. Everyone else assumed that this meant that they would have settled for a manslaughter verdict rather than go for a risky conviction. Roy leaned forward and mouthed, 'All right?' I nodded dully.

The probation officer said, 'You'll be all right, love. Didn't I tell you?'

It mattered little what he told me. There was only one thing left to be said now, and one person to say it. I stood as indicated to hear the verdict.

The jury forewoman rose and said, in a clear, strong voice, 'Guilty'. And the court was silent with shock, but not mine.

The next few minutes passed in a blur, until I heard the officer next to me whisper, was I going to faint? I said 'No, no.' The judge then said that he was sorry, but in view of the verdict he had no option but to sentence me to life imprisonment, that being the only permissible sentence for the conviction.

I heard the soft, shocked sobbing from the gallery behind me, but could not turn my head. All movement had to be carefully limited now to save precious energy. I was taken hurriedly downstairs to the cells and made to fill in forms with the necessary prison details to save time when we arrived. Roy, the consultant and the police surgeon came down to see me, but I had no words for them except a small measure of condolence for Roy, who was bemused, shocked, as I should have been. I thanked him woodenly before I was led to the van bound for London.

It was dark outside, that much I could tell dimly. I saw glimpses of things; the jurors rushing to their cars, glad to be away from the court to their awaiting husbands and wives and dinners. I felt the tiredness of so long released in me, spreading along inside my bones and confusing my thoughts. I watched neon lights intrude into the van as we flashed through Archway, along the Holloway Road, round the church, home. Home . . .

The officer who received me in the receptions hall informed me that I was shocked. 'In shock, dear, poor soul. Whatever did they give you life for?' I shook my head, unable to speak. I stood in the hallway while one officer took my details, another brought me a rough, hairy dressing gown that had seen better days, and yet another instructed me to strip and put on the garment. I did it all without feeling a thing, the swirling chaos of the receptions menagerie around me. All the procedures were familiar and I was able to undergo them without thought. Later, searched, bathed and numbered, I was checked by the prison doctor who took one look at me and wrote me up for a week's supply of sleeping medicine.

Soon I was taken upstairs to a little single cell in the hospital wing where I was to stay, for tonight. The door slammed fast and I sat on the hard bed, thankful for its unrelenting stoniness. I felt no desire whatsoever for sleep, or for daylight to appear. I spent that first night alternately staring out of the slits between the bars and walking round the little cell to stop me thinking. Thought would only bring tears, and incomprehension, and pain, and there was no room for such emotions in my self-built prison. All was bleak, and all was pain, and yet it was the pain that kept me going, sharp and fierce and pricking at my soul. It gave me something to clutch onto, to roll myself up with and cuddle against me. Mine. The way I felt then was all grey, a place I had come to where everything was one colour but without nuances of light or shade. Light I shrank from, light shed upon my bundle of misery and shame and fear and loathing of the creature that I now was. The darkness was so complete, so thick, so all-enveloping that it shrouded and withered me. It was a relief, and I let the tears roll silently down my face into the collar of my stiff-starched nightie, into the night.

Chapter Two

My grandmother had made her way from the west coast of Ireland to settle in the small town of Kenilworth in Warwickshire. Along the way she married my grandfather, a man about whom I know nothing except that he rarely spoke. In no time at all they had produced five children: Michael, Patrick, Josephine, Margaret and Elizabeth – my mother, who was born in 1925. A fervent churchgoer, my grandmother led the reluctant brood to Mass early every Sunday without fail, barely allowing for the intervention of natural disasters – bar death, of course, when a good Irish Catholic funeral-cum-wake would take place. A rather fierce woman, emotional and volatile, she had a quick temper which was just as instantly cooled and forgotten. Then she would be at a loss to understand why her children were cowering in the corner of the room, heads bent to avoid flying missiles. She had a heart as soft as muck, she would say, when needed. She was a sly old devil, fascinatingly different from her children. My mother, for instance, was not able to switch moods like Gran.

As the eldest girl, mother was unquestionably the one who bore the Glasswell family responsibilities after the two boys went off to the war in 1939. Working through the war in nearby Coventry as a secretary-cum-office manager in a large car firm, she gave nearly all her meagre salary to her mother; her sisters on the other hand, when they were grown up, did not have to do the same. Bitterness took hold of her then, but as a good Catholic daughter she kept it well hidden. The three sisters, years apart in age, were continents apart in outlook and attitude. It is almost impossible to convey an image of my mother in her youth, because of course I didn't know her, but we talked so often of her early life and spent so many evenings musing over the idiosyncrasies of her family that I felt and ached for her sensitivity as much as if I had been a part of it all myself.

My mother had been born with a restless spirit, and never really knew what it was she wanted – but she wanted better than she had now, that was for sure. She yearned to improve her status in life. I sensed the desires she must have had, and suppressed; to break free of the working-class mould that she had been born into, that had embittered her and given her a need to rise above it, to the class she felt she really, truly belonged to – to the bliss of middle-class bourgeoisie. But those sort of thoughts went unspoken, wistful and dreamy that they were.

She supposed, she told me, that she wanted, then, a husband and children. Wasn't every woman supposed to want those things? But beyond that, her dreams were hung up and left to dry, smelling of the hopes and wishes of the past, fragments of what might have been. She was different from her contemporaries in that she was not easily satisfied with what her mother and her mother's mother had taken for granted – the idea of existing solely as an accessory to a man, being always a daughter, a wife, a mother, and never a woman in her own right, a woman with dreams and hopes and ideals and aims. She knew that there must be something more, but never quite grasped hold of what it might be. Or perhaps she was afraid to.

When she left school at fifteen and went to work she discovered a side of her nature that could organize and take responsibility in the workplace. She left the anxieties and frustrations of her home life where they belonged, and threw herself into her work, making herself indispensable. At this time the male workforce was obviously somewhat depleted, and many women, my mother amongst them, began to realize their potential and abilities as business-women and decision makers. Previously programmed to become shadows of their mothers, they had now been given a new and awesome choice about their fate. Coventry, being an industrial city, was heavily bombed, but the war years were not fearful or worrying for my mother; for her it was a time of excitement, self-discovery and opportunity. The best years of her life, she often said, wistfully, nostalgically. They were to be her few years of happiness.

Coventry hummed with the excitement of thousands of milling GIs, who may well have been oversexed, overpaid and thoroughly unpopular with their English rivals, but were also the greatest fun. My mother fell for an extraordinarily handsome American called Bob, who had classic movie star looks. He captivated her with his charming and chivalrous manner, which was unusual in a soldier. Later, she often mused on how such a gentle man fared in the thick of the fighting. My mother never knew if he had even survived the war. As a child, looking at the worn but dazzling photos of him, I marvelled at his beauty and wondered whether, if he was still alive, he had suffered the fate of so many Americans, reduced to wandering around Stratford-on-Avon sporting a large behind clad in loud checked trousers. Spending her evenings taking out the various snaps of Bob and pondering his fate offered a romantic escape from the fearful banality of her life as wife and mother.

Meanwhile, life continued in wartime Kenilworth. My mother was still a virginal Catholic girl – unworldly, yet sophisticated enough to know that she needed to find a good and dutiful husband. American servicemen were categorically *not* husband material, unless you wanted to end up living in a shack in the wilds of Ohio, as some unfortunate GI brides found themselves doing.

It was not until after the war that my mother met William Reynolds, the man she was eventually to marry. He came from a poor but respectable, solidly working-class Birmingham family. When his father was killed in the First World War his mother had been left with four young sons to bring up alone. Bill and his mother had eventually settled in Kenilworth, after the three older boys had married. Mrs Reynolds was not the warmest, sweetest person in my father's world, but he had a great sense of loyalty and he remained with her until he married my mother.

From 1940 onwards he had been a submariner, where he learned to conquer fears such as claustrophobia. The experience must, I think, have been very similar to that of a prison cell – but so very much worse, with the ever-present threat of death heavy in the stale underwater air. It was from those deep-sea excursions that my father contracted the illness which lasted all his life. A substance called phosgene, a colourless, poisonous gas which was present in the submarines, settled on many of the submariners' lungs in a similar way to asbestos. From exposure to this substance my father acquired his grey-toned skin and the racking cough which was his constant companion. The stress and tension of life in submarines later drove him to the point of exhaustion and the summit of fear – once there, he rallied and seemed to be chasing thoughts that rested far inside his head. He often used to frown so deeply that it would raise great furrows on his forehead, and I would think him to be in pain, but it was only his elusive memories once again.

My father and his war-time comrades had been stretched to the limits of their endurance, down under the deep blue sea, encapsulated in their underwater jail. One of the long-term effects it had on my father was to give his life a special sense of urgency, a desperateness much the same as the feeling on release from prison. He seemed to be always on the edge of waiting for the day when they would want to take his freedom away again.

After the war he came home, mentally scarred and physically broken, but alive. Before the war he had been a mechanic by trade, so he went back to engineering in a city firm. Spending his days in the strenuous atmosphere of a very physical job, he found new life in painting, full of peace and sobriety by contrast.

Meanwhile, my mother was still occasionally seeing men who were returning from the war. Brought up in a very working-class home, she had higher aspirations than most, inspired by poverty and shame to climb out of the quagmire she felt herself to be in. She wished desperately to lift herself into a middle-class existence, and blamed the triviality of her days on her background. Wanting to meet the kind of man who would be able to build her a life in the social niche to which she felt she belonged, she was restless and unhappy. Around this time of her life, her early twenties, she suffered from several nervous breakdowns. These were due partly to the stressful situation at home, with a fractious, demanding mother and brothers and sisters whom she felt were selfish in letting her carry the whole family responsibility, including the biggest financial burdens, and partly to the lack of any real hope that her lot would ever be a happy one.

Then Bill turned up, wanting to find a wife, and being an impatient man he didn't want to wait too long before he settled down. No psychologist is needed to examine his desire for an immediate family: his own childhood had been a sad one, growing up to find that the war had stolen his father, which had rendered his mother bitter and reproachful. During his own war service he had had no home, nothing or no one to call truly his own. Now that he had the chance to change all that, he was determined to do so.

He was a very handsome man in a strange, intense manner. He appeared silent, even taciturn, had a brooding, darkly tinted face; green eyes, as mine are, in a deep-furrowed brow; a straight, long nose and that grey, crinkled skin that seemed to have been much used; and wide lips, with almost wolf-like teeth. Very thin and wiry after the deprivations of the war, he once dryly described himself to me as 'well-worn secondhand goods'. He looked, in short, as unlike the clean-cut GI image as possible.

He was intrigued by my mother's air of dignity and seeming haughtiness; she saw him as the white knight who could, if persuaded, whisk her away from reality on his petrol-engined charger (he had a motorbike at that time) to the promise of a better life. But my father had other ideas. He wanted a wife, and he wanted that wife to do wifely things – cook the meals, keep the house clean and organize the household finances. What he did *not* want was a wife who would look upon him as the catalyst for changing her lifestyle. Maybe they never compared notes on what each was expecting from marriage.

Bill didn't want a working wife, and in some ways this suited my mother because she was not over-ambitious, despite her obvious competence in the business world. What she hoped for more than anything was that whoever she married would take her away from her home to a better house, a better standard of living and a different social sphere. She wanted to get out of Kenilworth, where the neighbours knew all about her and the ignominies of her family life.

They launched into a whirlwind courtship fuelled not by romance, although there may have been an element of that at the very beginning, but by necessity. Dad wasn't prepared to waste time looking round for a wife, and my mother despaired of finding 'her man' if she hung around too much longer. Even she must have realized that in a small town she could only choose from a very limited number of men, most of whom she had known from childhood, from church and from events organized by the Catholic community – terribly virginal dances and non-alcoholic drinks parties. So it seemed, no doubt, like the best deal they could both get, and thus their fate was set.

They married, both of them beautiful in the wedding pictures – my father solemn-eyed, my mother pale and thoughtful in a mist of lace and trailing flowers. But Dad looks old, for the war years had eroded his features into permanent creases of anger, frustration and pain. He looks tired and wearied by the show and fuss of the wedding ceremony, and seems at odds with the pained artificiality that guests at a marriage inevitably convey. My aunts pose awkwardly as bridesmaids, gauche in their long-legged adolescent attire; my grandmother is a picture of Irish immortality, her silent husband beside her smiling at the camera in a vague, benign manner, probably longing to be at home with his pipe and paper.

Nobody knew quite what to make of my father, so alien was he to the ways of the Glasswell family. He never had the habit of analysing every thought, word and deed as did his new family, of sitting round the huge scrubbed wooden table in the steamy, bustling kitchen and talking the world to rights. Neither did he want to discuss, for hours at a time, art, literature and philosophy – my mother's family may have been at what she regarded as a low social echelon, but there was never any poverty in ideas or culture. Dad had his own passions and did not see the need to be 'always always talkin''. (My grandfather was much the same, and developed his capacity to stay silent for so long throughout life in a family of women who never ceased talking.) My parents' marriage was a mixed one in the truest of senses, and was doomed to failure from almost the very beginning; but the partners battled on and presented a sweet and sunny exterior to the world.

My father developed his life into a pattern of work and art. He found the same sense of satisfaction from his mechanical engineering job, which produced visible results, as he did from his painting – which may sound slightly patronizing. However he never intended, much less desired, that his pictures should make him famous or bring him financial reward – simply that they should continue to give him pleasure and be the source of relaxation that they were. He painted my mother, and later on, me, a smiling, golden-curled tot in a blue-ribboned frock. At one fateful point he grew dissatisfied with his lack of technical knowledge and enrolled for a series of art classes at the local library. These were not a success. At one class he sat astonished and speechless as the teacher put on a tape of jazz music and exhorted the class to 'move your brush as the music makes you'. Dad moved himself from the classroom, and never returned.

So he set himself a goal, to teach himself how to paint in oils, to draw with charcoals and pastels. Learning from the work of the Impressionists, he emulated the paintings of Renoir, Monet and Manet, loving with an artistic passion the dresses of the women, the colours of the Renoir-women's Titian locks, the reflections of light and shade that brought the Impressionistic canvases to life.

It is possible that due to the long and rather odd gap between my parents' marriage and my birth, my father saw his paintings, his creations, as his babies.

I don't even know if he ever yearned for a child. He was not the sort of man to want a son desperately, since there was no Reynolds dynasty; nor was he an emotional or tactile man. Like my mother, he was uncomfortable with displays of emotion and embraces and fond kisses, and did not know how to express his love for me; yet he loved me with a dim and distant fervour that lacked nothing because of its vagueness.

For a long and painful time I wondered and agonized over the possibility that I might be adopted – my parents seemed sometimes to be unsure of how to behave with me, as if I were a strange but interesting creature that had suddenly appeared in their middle-aged midst. And that, I suppose, was the crux of the problem. When I popped on to the scene in 1968, my mother was forty-three and my father fifty-two. They had been married for over eighteen years without a child, and while a couple in their twenties can expect to cope with a toddler, a couple in the midst of their mid-life crises must have found a crying, demanding babe incredibly hard to adjust to.

Another problem was that, while Dad was not prepared to make great changes to his lifestyle simply so that my mother could move up the social ladder, he did accept that she would be reasonably content if she had enough money to dress herself attractively, and decorate the house as she wanted. Then a funny thing happened – me. And they started to realize that babies are expensive to have and to bring up.

What an incredible difference it must have made to their previously peaceful lifestyle to have a small, wailing third party in the house. Mum soon discovered that I not only cost a lot of money to clothe and feed and generally keep running, but that I also cost her a lot in energy expenditure. Maybe she thought that she would be as good at organizing babies as she had been with offices: not necessarily so, of course.

I was a good baby, I am told – apart from the surprising loudness of my shrieks. Although I rarely cried, and had no discernible temper, when frightened or upset I produced a wail that could be heard the length and breadth of our street. I became famous for it. I never won a bonny baby contest, but I would certainly have won the prize for the loudest wailer in Kenilworth. But I *was* a good baby. Everyone loved me, neighbours queued up to look after me, strangers chucked me under the chin and old men dandled me on their knees. This last I did not like at all and would indicate my displeasure by a look of stubborn rage. Mum, if she saw the Look in time, would hastily whip me off the knee I was on to avert a wet disaster.

Although I had arrived as a surprise, I perhaps appeared just in time to fill the gap in Mum's life. I soon picked up the air of unfulfilled dreams and frustration that lingered like resentment in the house, and so imbibed the expectations which lay in waiting for me as I grew older. I realized with the intuition of childhood untainted with wisdom and commonsense analysis, that I was to be the achiever, the academic, the star who would outshine the others of my generation . . . wistful, unspoken wishes invested in me at a soft, impressionable age. At first, I thrived on this atmosphere of hopeful planning, not understanding the pressures it would heap upon me in later years.

I was unaware of the tenuous nature of the links that held my parents together, even though I was one of them. My birth sealed something between them, an acknowledgement of their marriage vows. For my mother it must have meant the fulfilment of the Catholic ideal – the purpose of sex being the procreation of children. Like my grandmother, she was a fervent and regular churchgoer, and a firm believer in the rules and ethics of the Church. I doubt that she could have agreed intellectually with the explanations for some of the decrees – those concerning sex and the role of women – but she had been brought up to accept without question, and, uneasily, she did.

The years up to my first taste of school were fairly uneventful, bar certain incidents that were partially responsible for my mother's neurotic nature. As a very young baby I tried to walk before I could crawl, and promptly fell over on to the heavy stone fireplace, giving my skull a crack. I set up such a wail as had never been heard before – even from me – and was taken to hospital, where they put me back together again.

By the age of four and a half I had developed a wide vocabulary, thanks to Mum's determination that I should be fully equipped with all possible verbal defences. Her strategy worked, but to her disadvantage. In the local grocer's shop one day I saw a fat lady – an enormously fat lady. Never before had my young eyes seen such a sight, and I announced this to the world in tones anything but dulcet. No amount of furious hisses or threats of sore bottoms could deter me from asking the unfortunate victim just exactly why she was so large. Later, at home, a stony silence ensued as a result of the embarrassment I had caused. Piqued, I piped up: 'Well, I only wanted to know why. And you told me to always be sure to ask why things are the way they are.' This was entirely true. I had been subtly instructed to analyse, question, examine, ask why, and where, and what for – but doubtless in a more diplomatic manner. I changed my tack, and in future asked why in a lower voice.

At my local infants' school I demonstrated talents of a peculiar kind. A small boy called Nigel became smitten with me, not for my long curly hair or innocent green eyes, but for my ability to neigh like a horse. Nigel and I were, it seemed, doomed in love. Two days before my sixth birthday, he blindfolded me and instructed me to run round the playground (I forget exactly what the point of this game was). Effectively blind, I ran straight as a die into the nearest stone wall, breaking my arm. Nigel was the recipient of many black looks from that day on.

This catalogue of incidents grew as I did. There was an unpleasant episode when, aged eight or nine, I was playing with one of Dad's collection of watches. He had confided to me that one of his ambitions was to own an armful of watches and wear them all at once. Having inherited two from a distant relative, he had incautiously allowed me to play with them. As I sat on the stairs, Mum descended and said with reprimand in her voice, 'You'll break those if you play with them.' I dropped one of the watches down over the staircase on to the hall floor below. Accidentally. All Hell broke loose.

Two months later I was a budding Cinderella. Peeking behind the door to the school stage, I wound my hand around the jamb in my excitement. A little horror, watching me, came up and pulled the door to. My thumbnail promptly parted company with my thumb, and a wail of pain and shock rose to meet the assembled proud parents in the waiting audience beyond the door.

From a very early age I remember going to Mass every Sunday and saint's day, all through Easter and, of course, all through Christmas. I never considered any other way of spending a Sunday morning, in fact. The whole thing was bound up with guilt – guilt if you didn't go to Mass (neglecting your duties), and guilt if you went but whilst there thought unseemly thoughts. I lived in fear of sneezing in the hushed silence of the church, or of being caught exchanging glances with one of my friends who also had to attend Mass. Neither did I dare to do anything as disrespectful as wearing jeans to Mass, because, I was told crossly, God might see me and think it a lack of respect on my part. I used to think how damn lucky God would be if I were to want to wear my brand-new jeans to church.

In due course I entered into the full spirit of the Catholic enterprise. I became in turn a Brownie and a Guide, and went on all the outings organized by the church. This was not a bundle of fun: it involved going on retreats to Stone, in Staffordshire, where I spent a fortnight every summer on my knees in reluctant and resentful prayer. Horribly fascinated by the beards and whiskery old faces of the silent nuns who ran the place, I prayed that I would not have to become a nun. I sallied forth on these journeys with glassy-eyed anticipatory visions of boredom. Growing amid the stoicism of the Irish-Catholic community around me, my parents were contradictory in their beliefs. My father went to church whenever he pleased, which was not, consequently, very often. He went twice a year, on holiday, where he was safe from the zealots of the church in Kenilworth who would chastise irregular worshippers for their lack of consistency. My mother was the opposite in her religious outlook. Years of conditioning and forceful, rigorous environment had stifled any protests she might have had about her faith.

At one time my mother went to Mass daily, to pray for the souls of the dearly departed (which, in our family, were plentiful). At Lent we fasted, and dutifully deprived ourselves of some little pleasure to satisfy the Church ruling that 'All good Catholics must give something up at Lenten; to be offered up to God, for the good of their souls.' I gave up playing with my Cindy dolls, and using Mum's nail varnish without permission, and eating bubble gum. Mum gave up eating sweets, and smoking. Dad, a Protestant and rare churchgoer, snorted and said that in his opinion we were in need of a doctor, not a priest. This was almost certainly true.

At the age of seven I had been sent to Catholic school which professed to teach the catechism. It was a mile and a half away from home, and I hated it as a child *can* hate a school. (It was a wonderful relief to have, at last, such a clear and uncomplicated hatred of a building and a system; far nicer than hating a person – which might, after all, invoke the penalty of saying three Hail Marys and an Our Father.) Mainly I hated it because the head teacher was a dragon, sent straight from the jaws of Hell to persecute little children – or so it seemed. She was also the mother of my best friend, and the whole class were united in unspoken sympathy for their young colleague.

After what were for me two tear-filled and fairly miserable years I and my fellow Catholics moved on to another RC school, two bus rides away from home. The new place was bigger, brighter, modern and colourful; we liked it, and felt more anonymous in the mass of children surging from all directions. There was an air of workmanlike efficiency about the place, and I felt that here I would progress in my learning. At this age I had already made a career decision: I was going to become a writer and an artist (I could not be content with only one prospective profession). At home I would sit in an adjacent room drawing while my father sat in the sitting room painting, me trying to chew the pencil in exactly the same way that he chewed at the brush when temporarily lacking inspiration.

I soon encountered the school bully, a child of deceptively angelic appearance who seemed to be a cross between Crystal Tips, and the Wicked Witch of the West from *The Wizard of Oz*. She delighted in practising tortuous forms of mental cruelty upon me, sensing me to be weak, over-sensitive and easily reduced to tears. She spirited my few friends away from me, pinched and bit me in the classroom, and waited for me to appear around corners, when she would bid everyone run away from me. I began to suffer badly from headaches, almost every day, which would be blinding by the end of the last lesson and would make me long for home. After a year of this, I was also suffering from paranoia, and did the unforgivable thing in playground rules – went home and told Mum, amidst rivulets of tears. She went, cold-lipped, to the class teacher, who turned to the headmaster – the buck stopped there. Yes, they said shamefacedly, they had noticed the bullying. Yes, they had turned a blind eye. Well, they thought it might be that she disliked me because she thought I was 'common', in other words that I came from a poor family – my father only earned a low wage, and they had taken on a mortgage before they had the expense of a child.

The other girls who had followed the bully's lead now came to me, chastened by my pallor and dark-ringed eyes and also by the headmaster's stern words to them. They put their arms about me, gave me little gifts and stroked my hair – but I could not be won round. I was far too disillusioned about human nature and I wondered if this was how grown-ups were, following-their-leader and unable to act as thinking, feeling individuals. I wanted apologies, some demonstration that I was not really so horrid to be with, but they were at a loss to know what they had done. The ringleader, she who shall remain nameless, had coerced them into obedience: weak characters following a stronger one. We children were nine years old then, but I felt ancient. My mother and I looked at each other in ironic contemplation when the telephone rang and we were offered weepy apologies from one of the girls' mothers.

Why did I encounter such a fierce antagonism? Perhaps because my father was, in their eyes, 'common' (read working-class); and because my mother, they sneered, was 'weird' (read 'aspiring', or 'wishfully thinking upwardly mobile'). Perhaps because we were poor – maybe they thought poverty was infectious. And perhaps because I was aloof, holding back from the giggling gaggles of girlies in the playground, and chose instead to immerse myself in literature – a dream world of my own to float away to. When I was very young, my mother taught me the value of words wisely and sparingly used, spoken, written, thought – knowing that a sensitive child would need some defence against the world. She may also have realized how books would be a kind of salvation to me. Around the house in plentiful heavy wooden cases were old favourites such as Dickens, Jane Austen, Tolstoy, Eliot. There were countless volumes of poetry – Tennyson, Browning, Keats, Blake, Shelley. My mother loved the fiction of the Victorian era and truth from the Regency, the period in which she would, she felt, have been so much at home.

We shared many things. Often our sense of frustration with our lack of cash took us on lengthy shopping expeditions in nearby Leamington or Coventry – mostly wistful window-gazing, combined with occasional brief forays into cheap shops to snap up bargains. My mother seemed made to wear expensive, well-cut clothes, for she had a style and a presence that made her stand out in any gathering. She longed desperately to buy smart, fashionable garments, but our budget would not have stretched to designer hosiery, let alone £200 jackets. So, in consolation, we scoured the secondhand shops and the back-of-a-lorry market stalls, and had great fun finding some real bargains. We would break our day with a cup of real coffee (the treat) in a real coffee shop, and then fight our way on to the bus home. We would return laden with bags of cut-price goodies and I, impulsive and impatient, would rush upstairs to try my share on, parading in front of the speckled gilt mirror.

Dad must not know – it was our conspiracy. We had a tiny piece of gentle, rare fun, when he would stare at an old, tat-ridden skirt of mine, and demand, 'When d'you buy that, then? Been spending my money again?' but would not notice when, trembling with delicious curls of fear, I appeared in a new outfit. He was intimidating in his own way – a silent, slightly threatening strength that rarely manifested itself except as exasperation. As a child, I could have wound him around my little finger if I had been manipulative, but I was blissfully ignorant of such machinations and our relationship ran fairly smoothly because we were honest with each other.

Since we were so short of money Dad grudgingly allowed Mum to go back to work, in a local shop selling Spanish ceramics. She soon progressed from mere shop assistant to doing the books and then the buying, and eventually was made manager. Sales shot up with welcome rapidity, due to Mum's winning ways with the customers. Now the pressure of being the sole breadwinner was taken off Dad. His staunch ideas about his wife staying at home changed when the situation became really desperate, and I think even he must have realized how little she was having to manage on per week.

When I was about eight or nine I developed a passion – an obsession, shall we say – for riding lessons. I was told in no uncertain terms to forget that sort of idea; horses were only for the rich and idle, Dad grunted. As stubborn as he, I refused to abandon the idea and resolutely set about making enough money to pay for this extravagance. Starting in truest entrepreneurism, I washed the neighbours' cars, walked their dirty, mud-caked dogs, soothed their shrieking babies and dug their gardens. This was very good for my energy output but not nearly enough to pay for the equestrian activities I so longed for. So off I marched to the local stables and begged for a job. No, said the owner, a toothy woman with a shelf-like bosom and a large, horsey backside. Too young, too small.

Eventually, a miracle happened in the shape of a small lady from our local church, who had a pony that would be just what I needed to learn on, she informed me. Ignorance is bliss. I sighed and plumped for lessons on Flower – a short, squat black creature with hyperthyroid eyes and large, bursting nostrils – rather than none at all. For £1 per week, which I earned by cleaning Flower and her stable, I was permitted to seat myself on her broad rump and walk sedately around the little field. She would not shift herself from a walking pace without a great deal of foolish but necessary 'Grrrr' sounds from me.

As I approached puberty, I became more aware of how different my family were from other children's. Mine seemed odder, more eccentric than the others'. I wondered why. Funnily enough, the obvious age difference between my parents never occurred to me, and yet it was evident to all my contemporaries, who, some years later, told me how strange they thought our family triangle was. My parents rarely put in an appearance at school events, despite the fact that parents' days and sports days are the times when most fond mums and dads turn out to gaze proudly at their offspring. Mine did not, usually because Dad would be working, and in any case wouldn't go to events that involved being sociable to large numbers of people, and because Mum didn't like the fact that these affairs were always out of town or in the evening, and for many years we had no reliable transport. We were too proud to ask for or accept a rarely proffered lift, as we could not reciprocate. So school social occasions left me aimlessly wandering the corridors and winding up in the library with a book. Consequently, my friends never saw my mother and father. On the few occasions that I did invite them home with me I felt an enormous pull of divided loyalties between my parents and my puzzled, curious and often rude friends.

My grandmother played no small part in the farcical life of my family. I dreaded going to see her, always on edge awaiting her terse commentary on my growth, educational ability (or lack of it) and general behaviour. Old and garrulous, she would peer at me, narrow-eyed, and exclaim, 'Lord! But you're a streelish chile.' 'Streelish' was my grandmother's eccentric term for gangly, or for someone wearing long, draggy skirts, in which case they would be called a streeleen. I was then a tall, thin child, all coltlike dangling legs. These pronouncements would be made in a strong Irish brogue – no thin querulousness of old age for her. I thought she would surely live forever.

She still had the power to terrify most of the family and the odd neighbour who got in her way. One day, out shopping (these trips took several hours since she invariably met someone to gossip with, and then would return home, exhausted, having quite forgotten the shopping) she had taken the errant family dog, named Pidge, with her. A neighbour, bicycling past, swerved violently to avoid him as he ran out into the road and fell off. My grandmother was not impressed. Convinced it had been the cyclist's fault, she took off her hat and, mentally rolling up her sleeves, harangued the astonished woman for riding without due care and attention. By the time she had done, the neighbour was sure it *had* been all her fault. Returning home, Pidge was fed best steak for shock, and Gran related the tale to other neighbours in an injured and highly aggrieved manner.

Once, visiting her on a hot summer afternoon, we went to the back door as usual and found her slumped over in her chair, a bottle marked 'paint stripper' by her side. It transpired that she had been keeping her chest medicine in an old paint stripper bottle – God alone knows why, and perhaps even He did not bargain for such eccentricity as hers. Mum panicked. Out came the mustard and the milk, and down my unfortunate, bewildered and, for the first time in her life, silent grandmother's throat in an attempt to induce vomiting. Nothing happened except a lot of uncertain heaving. I timidly suggested salt – we tried this, and a thin trickle of fluid came out of her mouth. Eventually all three of us went off in an ambulance, Gran prone on the stretcher, Mum and me bemused by the whole operation.

Gran recovered, but her chest condition grew worse, and not long afterwards she died as quietly as could have been hoped. By this time my mother's nerves and health had deteriorated badly – she had been trying to cope with looking after Gran during her illness, looking after my father, also frequently ill, as well as caring for me and running the household as usual. The remainder of the family were strangely absent from the scene. At the time, I couldn't understand why she didn't cry at the funeral. On reflection, I doubt if she would have had time for tears, or the energy that real grieving demands.

Mum had already been diagnosed as a neurotic, and she now developed a thyroid condition which entailed many visits to hospital. One of my strongest memories is of the local outpatients' department, where I would be fed chocolate biscuits by kind nurses in sly anticipation of outbursts of tears – they were used to such things, but I was stauncher, and was duly rewarded by a visit to the doctors' room to be shown how the stethoscope worked, and all manner of wonderful treats reserved for good children who did not cry at seeing their mummies being jabbed by sharp needles. Mum had so much blood taken that I was worried she might not have enough left to live on, but the doctor laughed and told me that blood replaces itself rapidly. Mum herself could not bear to watch the procedure, but for inquisitive me it was all an adventure.

At certain times in my childhood it seemed that one or other of my parents was ill with increasing and chilling regularity. Dad was working too hard; as well as his full-time job, which was almost certainly too strenuous for him, he had taken on the responsibility of an old lady who was a friend of Mum's. From a background of gentry who had fallen on hard times, she was not exactly living in poverty; but she was certainly lonely and isolated. All her family were dead and she herself had never married; instead she had become the archetypal Victorian old maid, kept at home to be housekeeper to her brothers. Dad set up a pattern of calling in on his way home from work, even in the depths of winter with the unreliable car we now possessed. When the car was out of commission he cycled to work and back, but never forgot to pop in to see her. He would find himself trapped for at least an hour by her stilted talk, as rusty words tumbled from the lips of one obviously pitifully unused to company and to modern life. She talked dreamily of days gone by and seemed not to know the date or even the year. Alone, and confused in an alien world of changing generations, she touched my father's heart. Impatient with fools and intolerant of avoidable weaknesses, he was the softest of men when faced by those with a genuine problem.

But the effort began to tell in lines of strain on his grey face. He had a heart condition, something I'd been vaguely aware of since I was old enough to take in the words. I was unsure exactly what a heart condition was; it was never explained to me, and my inquisitive questions were fobbed off with evasive non-answers. Ever ready to eavesdrop, I listened at doors, and simply soaked up all unwelcome and threatening information like an unhappy little sponge. Looking through medical books at school, I began to see why the trivial differences in our eating arrangements were so; our diet revolved totally around what Dad was, and wasn't, allowed to eat. We were none of us ever great carnivores, but any evidence of cow or piggy in our house brought on a bout of frenzied chopping away of fat. No gold top milk here, but always Marvel, even for us, in case Dad cheated and used our milk; and my father, much to his disgust, became a Flora man. All this was to try to ward off the risk of an angina attack. On early summer mornings we sat, Dad and I, on the back doorstep, eating cornflakes and skimmed milk companionably side by side. No words were spoken; we just sat watching the sun rise higher above the tree-filled horizon. I had no real love for cornflakes but wanted to keep Dad company, and if he had to eat the small orange crunchy things, then so must I.

After work and at weekends I would sit watching him paint, tongue held between his yellowing teeth, or working on whichever of his succession of beloved cars he owned at that particular moment. He lavished much tender care on these vehicles, but they rarely went more than a few yards before chugging to a sad and ignominious halt in the middle of the street. I felt safe and secure, womb-like, in the atmosphere of his male preserves – the aroma of cigar smoke, and his flat cap and greatcoat hung on the garage door.

I worried particularly about him when he turned ashen after a particularly strenuous weekend spent trying to erect an extension on our little house. My mother was determined to have one, and to please her Dad sweated in the heat of the drought summer of 1976. Over the walled boundaries of our garden lay the town's Catholic cemetery, the view from my window. I often stood, wakeful in the night, listening to the sound of my father's pain-filled, restless sleep in the next room. I looked out over the grey shapes in the moonlit misty night, lumps of stone encrusted with garish wreaths, and sighed, then climbed back into bed.

One spring, full of apricot and lime blossoms in the nearby field, both of my parents were ill. Mum had been rushed into hospital for a 'cut-throat' thyroid operation, and my father was also there with one of his vague 'heart conditions'. I was despatched to the nearest, if not dearest, aunt, my mother's sister, plus husband and two children. My uncle, Gordon, hated anyone at all staying in his house – even, I suspected, his own two daughters. He was a silent shroud of a man, morose and uncommunicative.

Not knowing what to do with this spare little person, Aunt Peggy took me to a local café which was the proud possessor of a toucan called Percy, who would utter cheeky phrases in an apologetic, depressed monotone, wild black eyes peering myopically at his visitor, seeming to be ashamed of his part in representing that species. I felt weepily sorry for him, and took to trotting along daily to feed him a chocolate eclair which my luckless aunt had procured at some expense for me.

While staying at my aunt's house, I laboured greatly to produce a 'Get Well' card for Mum (not for Dad – I wasn't supposed to know that he was ill). Confected out of quantities of fabric, glitter, paints and tinsel, on reflection it must have looked a real dog's dinner. I don't know how Mum would have received it without being undiplomatic. As it was, she didn't receive it at all in its original state because the unpopular Gordon became more so by (accidentally) throwing my lovely, lovely card on the fire, thinking it to be litter. I was furious. I rescued what I could, and, crying smoky tears, took my burnt offering to the hospital.

The slimness of our family income over the years, even when Mum was working as well, meant that we learned the fine art of stretching a small, pathetic joint of beef over several days, and took great care to stumble around in the dark and wash in cold water to save on electricity. This did not mean that I had a deprived childhood – I guess it was even good for me. I learnt never to ask for or expect pocket money, but went out to earn for myself as soon as anyone would employ me. A bag of sweets was a treat to be savoured, not something to be expected.

However, the strain of such constant penny-pinching and agonizing over bills imposed a pressure on my parents' relationship. Never a happy household, it became a place of silent, menacing unrest. I had always been a withdrawn, detached child, due to the insular nature of our family life, and now I drank in the atmosphere between my parents. They were, after all, my role models. Neither of them had any real friends, except Dad's adopted old lady, so the house was empty of fresh voices or healthy laughter. Mum had no one to discuss the state of the world with like she used to do at home when she was a girl, and Dad preferred his own company anyway. They had slept in separate rooms for as long as I could remember. I had long since ceased bringing friends home, or visiting them since I couldn't reciprocate, and so we all became individual entities rather than a family. Mum did things about the house most of the time, clattering in the kitchen to mask the screaming silence. Dad would be in the garage or painting his latest work of art, while I would be following him around, or in my room thinking about it all. I spent an inordinate amount of time just thinking about the future of the family. I shrank into myself and drew upon my store of reserves, clutching at the rapidly diminishing folds of security, feeling the chill as my blanket of comfortable normality was stripped away. The edges of warm, family life and safety (in my theories, gleaned from books, these were to me synonymous) seemed to be slipping away.

My parents rarely spoke to each other but communicated their messages through me, since there were certain things that Mum grudgingly had to include Dad in, and vice versa. I felt some anger at both of them for each making the other so needlessly unhappy, but dared not speak out for fear of being the one who sparked off the final explosion. I became their runner, then, not understanding how they could maintain such silence, and feeling my mother's wrath as it turned on me. I would be instructed, coldly, as the culpable one, loving Dad as I did, 'Go and tell your father that his dinner is ready.' Back and forth, like an office lackey. 'Tell your mother that I don't want any bloody dinner.' I seemed to lose my identity as a child and became, in their eyes, someone mature and capable of comprehending a situation that even they could not fathom.

So the onset of adulthood arrived early, a crash course, in those silent days. Trivialities became matters worth a verbal fight (there was never any physical violence in our home, but I'm sure the desire must have been there on both sides). Words were rare and precious gems to be exchanged in sour confrontations, when my parents broke their silence to voice a carefully nurtured grievance. They both became progressively bitter, at each other's failings and at the world. I heard both sides as a mute listener, there as a handy ear into which they could release their pent-up outpourings.

Terrified that this state of play would mean the end of us as a family (I didn't bargain for the die-hard Catholic ruling against divorce), I became more introverted and frozen at school, looking through haunted eyes as I watched other children come in morning after morning red-eyed and sniffling. Everyone's parents seemed to be divorcing; and I was sure mine were. I lived in constant dread of being sat down and told, 'There is something we have to tell you.' It never happened, but the cold, palpable silence remained, continued, deepened. I cried every night, noiselessly, for fear of being heard and having to voice and realize my thoughts.

Chapter Three

We now had separate lifestyles for the two distinct halves of our little, disintegrating family. Dad was a natural lone wolf, and Mum felt trapped, locked into the world she despised, locked out of the elusive world she longed to enter, that of dignified sessions of morning coffee, elegant, expensive clothes, and dinner parties. Our annual family holiday was still going ahead, though, and this cheered me a little; if this stalwart monument to togetherness (closeted in a tiny flatlet) still existed, there must be hope for the marriage. Our place of vacation, always and without fail, was Weston-super-Mare, a little run-down seaside town near Bristol. I loved it, and felt a sorry sympathy with it precisely because it was run-down and scruffy. The attractions for a child were not great, but it was fairly deserted even in the peak months of summertime, and I walked along the lonely, mudstuck sands with Dad, companionably silent, both of us deep in our worried thoughts, with our unconsciously identical frowns. Dad had a routine there, to end the evening walk with a bag of fat, browned chips from the noisy pier. I worried a little about the black bits nestling amongst the chips, but since Dad ate them fast and with relish, my fastidious fears were allayed.

We spent so little time together, yet it was all the more precious and valuable for that reason. We talked rarely and touched never, not even a goodnight kiss, but communicated in an unspoken depth where we recognized each other. Although I had, and still have, many of my mother's qualities, I am singularly like Dad in subtler ways. I guess that on holiday he might have enjoyed the company of a son more, to share 'manly' activities with, but to please him I sank intuitively into the role of a boy, without losing sight of reality.

He liked to think he had a daughter who was not dirt-shy, and, sliding into my androgynous role, my hair short, always in trousers and shapeless T-shirts, I looked the part. I had no tomboy desires – in fact, I loved dresses and pretty things – but I was happy to be whatever he wanted. Dad went to church here, his twice-yearly trip to the modern Anglican building in the town, while Mum and I worshipped in the large old Catholic church on the hill, where the priest's accent was soft with a West Country lilt.

It was no holiday for my mother. She hated the place venomously and felt it to be reeking of poverty, working-class hopelessness and 'the best that people could afford'. Life there was no different for her. She shopped, cleaned the flat and cooked meat and three veg meals for my father (a great traditionalist where food was concerned. He would never take a holiday abroad, he stated, because he 'couldn't be doing with nasty messy foreign food'.) She did not like the sun, and covered her body up from the weak, scanty rays of the English sun with unnecessary fervour.

As for me, I fell in love with a pony called Pinto, who haughtily stalked the beaches of Weston offering children rides as a change from seaside donkeys. Pinto was an unknown quantity, half New Forest and half we knew not what. For the sheer pleasure of being near him I persuaded the owner of the ponies to let me have the dubious job of walking them up and down the beach and holding their tiny charges on to them. Often a pleased parent, rescuing their offspring at the end of the short ride, would pat me on the head, and say 'Thanks, son.' I was not sure I liked this, which may be why all our holiday snaps showed me with a cross, scowling face. I badly wanted to take Pinto home at the end of the holiday and dropped all kinds of unsubtle hints to Mum and Dad about how easy it was to transport a small horse home to Kenilworth. Mum was dismissive, but Dad was exasperated: 'Bloody kid! When

I said you could have a holiday souvenir I didn't mean a pony.' He did, however, realize it represented my desperate need for 'something of my own' to love, and sensed my welling loneliness and gradual premature departure from childhood. Needless to say, Pinto and I parted company at the end of the fortnight, to shrieks and sobs on my part – and no great loss, I suppose, on his.

We returned home at the end of our holiday, the silence reinforced by the closeness of our environment, one large room which echoed whenever rare words were uttered. There had of course been no visible distractions of work, or other attention-deflecting devices. We carried on in this vein, trapped in the silence of frustration and confusion, never exchanging any real words.

That last holiday to Weston was in the summer of 1979. I spent most of the following winter immersed in the dining room with Dad who was attempting, a big step for him, to paint original work rather than copying other paintings. Studying a huge jam jar full of golden-creamy daffodils, tongue stuck out in fierce concentration, he worked into the night to produce his best effort. I squatted on the floor beside him, fascinated by the delicate brushstrokes, his long, bony fingers clutching the Daler board to steady his work.

The words 'heart condition', bandied about with increasing frequency, left me in a permanent state of worry. Neither Mum nor any of the rest of the family would explain to me exactly what the problem was. I suppose they thought it best not to threaten my world with the burden of such knowledge. I fretted a whole lot more not knowing what it was that was wrong with him. So Dad lay in various hospitals having the mysterious 'heart condition' while I developed a worried frown. I wasn't allowed to visit him – I was not supposed to know that he was ill. My vivid imagination ran completely wild, with visions of Dad in a coma, on his deathbed, with angel-faced nurses floating around, accompaniments to my usual nightmares, which came to me often. Mum had been told by doctors that any undue stress or upset could raise Dad's potential for an angina attack. One of the activities guaranteed to raise

Dad's temper, and thus his potential for an angina attack, was driving. God help those who drove in his path, or forgot to signal, or overtook him at a speedy pace. Once he decided we should do something unprecedented in our small family – take a trip together, all three of us. So off we set on what he gruffly informed us was a 'mystery tour'. We ended up in exotic Coventry city centre, all of seven miles away, Mum and I charitably smothering our protests and laughter as he asked us at regular intervals, 'Don't know where you're goin', do you? Ha!' Of course we did. We came this way on the bus all the time, but how could we spoil his attempt to patch things up and call a kind of truce? Mum confided in a whisper that, when they had been courting, he had taken her every Saturday on a 'mystery trip', and without fail they had always ended up in Banbury. At least, she smiled wanly, this trip *was* somewhere other than there.

However, car trips would have been incomplete without some input from Dad regarding the other drivers on the road. 'Bloody women!' he'd exclaim. 'Shouldn't be allowed out without their husbands. Dangerous in a car, these females are. Look at this one! Bloody fool! Get off the road!' All this would be accompanied by furious gestures out of the hastily wound down window. This would no doubt be normal practice in Bombay, but was rather less so in Warwickshire. When I put this to him, he looked darkly at me and told me that he had faintly Indian origins. There seemed to be no answer to this – he had in fact encountered racism during the war years due to his exotically dark skin, black hair and molten eyes.

Despite the pain it gave him when the angina set in, he could not prevent himself getting stressed and frustrated when in the driving seat. At one point he gave up and took to his bike. He could be seen of a morning, long, thin figure coiled tightly over the handlebars, rickety wheels wobbling precariously as he rode off into the wild grey yonder, singing at the top of his fine voice: 'Oh, what a wonderful feeling, oh what a wonderful day . . . .'

One day, Dad and I went off to Leamington for a pair of school shoes for me. Dad hated shopping with female company, so, when we arrived, he decided that rather than put himself through the agony of trailing around shoe shops he would go and pore over the art books in the bookshop and meet me back at the car at eleven o'clock. I took my time in the shops, and when I had finally chosen a pair, I realized it was already 11.45. I rushed back to the car, fearful of his wrath. It was a freezing February day, with remnants of the January snow still melting away, and he was stamping his feet against the frosty chill of the air, furious-faced, brow furrowed with worry. Too angry to speak, he remained silently fuming until we neared home. There had recently been reports of two local girls of my age abducted in daylight. Suddenly he turned to me: 'Where the bloody Hell have you been? Have you thought of how worried I've been? No, I suppose you haven't – too bloody vain and selfish like your mother.' He cursed the other drivers on the way home, fumed at their incompetence and drove too fast. His face was even then grey with pain, hands clenched on the wheel as if to hold himself upright.

When we got back to the house he flung himself straight into the 'study', the tiny bedroom he had used from the days when he and my mother began sleeping apart. I trailed miserably in to Mum in the front room, heavy with guilt and the weight of my selfishness. She looked weary, as if she had finally come to the end of something and had tussled with herself. I felt a fear rising in me that I could not explain or rationalize, but I remained silent amid the wreckage of my home and family.

Later that evening we sat around the television as usual. Dad ignored me. There was no question of him telling my mother about that morning's incident; he was a fierce anti-tale teller. Getting up from his chair to change TV channels, he turned a sickening shade of grey-blue around his lips. He fell heavily on to the floor, and my mother and I watched, paralysed, as he tried to speak, sweat beading on his forehead with effort. Galvanized into action, Mum screamed at me to call an ambulance. Trembling, I obeyed. Mum meanwhile was trying to stop Dad from moving at all – no easy task. After an eternity the ambulance arrived. We sat inside, petrified into immobility in the back of the blue-lit vehicle as it swayed through the streets of the little town, sirens wailing to an absent audience.

When we arrived at the hospital in Warwick we were taken to the doctors' room. Cups of tea, the English cure-all, were proffered but refused. Soon the doctor himself came, accompanied by his many minions (I suppose he was a surgeon but this medical hierarchy meant nothing to me). He had a slow, ponderous manner of releasing information, delivered in a flat, Home Counties monotone. We felt he would drive us mad, so slow and almost casual was he. There was, he said, no chance of a recovery this time. The heart had been worn so thin by previous angina attacks that the end was surely in sight. But then we had been told that it was only a matter of time, hadn't we? Watching Mum, I understood that she had known all along how imminent the chances of this were. Tears were threatening to squeeze themselves out of my sore eyes, which I rubbed with a grubby finger. The doctor leaned down to me and boomed in my ear that I was to be a 'good, brave girl like your Daddy is trying to be'.

Time flagged and dragged. We were weary, restless. I remember endless cups of coffee, and a constant stream of nurses who knew nothing but were blanket-sympathetic ('He'll be all right, child, don't look so worried') and stern-faced doctors who hurried by with their clipboards and their entourage. Different aromas assailed me – disinfectant, starched linen, sick. I thought of the hospital visits Mum and I had made for her numerous blood tests. I sat occupied with memory tricks, whilst Mum was stony, her hands frozen, her coffee untouched. We could not reach out to each other even in the midst of a shared crisis, but sank into our separate dream worlds instead.

Eventually we were told we could go and see him but were not to be frightened by all the appliances attached to him. God! I was eleven years old then, with a tendency to be a little alarmist. It was midnight now on the grimy hospital clock as we were ushered into the intensive care ward. I didn't cry, but stood in a block of ice that protected me from feeling what I should have felt. He was all wired up, still a bluey shade. I guess I had thought that the doctors would be able to magic him back to a state of normality . . . .

I went outside the ward just in time to be violently sick, to my great shame. I was shaking, and Mum was apologising for me, she white-faced at the sight of him, nerves ruffled by my presence. We were told that old chestnut: 'His condition is as stable as can be expected', and we would be allowed to stay overnight in the hospital 'just in case' – just in case of what, we were not told. I was well aware of what those words meant, however. We were taken to the little annexe built for such occasions where the nurse issued us with stiff cotton nighties and hard, wiry toothbrushes. We lay miserably on the high, lumpy hospital beds and tried to sleep, an impossible expectation. Mum did not mention Dad at all, perhaps too careful of her own sanity and mindful that sleep would help us to cope with whatever the morrow might bring.

The night seemed to end eventually and we woke, stiff and itchy from the starched sheets. The view from the window of the tiny kitchenette was of porters bringing in the night's casualties like so many carcasses to a butcher's shop. We were shepherded along to Dad's ward, now a special area for coronary patients. I still didn't know what had really happened. He was still bluey grey, but was awake and seemed almost cheerful. Tubes were connected to every part of his body, or so it seemed. He smiled vaguely at me and spoke in a low tone with Mum for a while, then everyone else in the room seemed to fade. He beckoned me forward. I crept closer, scared but filled with a painful, bursting love for him, so defenceless and white-gowned. He whispered to me that the nurses were 'terrors', and that they would not let him get out of bed (he was a terrible patient). 'Buggers, they are!' he exclaimed. His eyes were bright. Then he sobered and told me that I must look after Mum now, and properly – no more running off, he admonished with a wink. (This was in reference to the days when, in a paddy, I would announce that I was leaving home but could always be tempted back – 'Oh, you're leaving before your tea, then? And so I'll have that cake all to myself.')

Then, I was told to leave the bed as the doctor was due on his ward round.

By now it was eight-thirty and Mum insisted we get back home in time for me to put on my uniform and go to school. I was less keen, but a nurse offered us a lift to Kenilworth and off we went. After a dash for the bus I was among my schoolmates, but not at all inclined to tell them of the events of the night. My mind was not at school, but in the ward with my father. The hospital was just along the road from the school, and at lunchtime there I flew. On the ward, no one could tell me where he'd been moved to, or if he'd been sent home. The nurses were reticent with me – such a change from the night before – and I slunk away.

Rushing home, I stopped short as I flung my bag down in the hallway and saw Mum on the phone. 'His official documents and birth certificate will be on their way to you,' she was saying in a peculiar, clearly enunciated way. As she saw me she put down the phone and turned to me. At my demand of 'How is he? Can we go and visit him tonight?' she passed a hand over her pale face and said, 'No. No. He died this morning.'

I stood there, cold and immobile. She went into the kitchen, moving stiffly, like an old woman. We were two separate entities, not even able to come together in our grief. She spoke to me, but it seemed as though the words were moving through mud. She was asking me what I wanted for my tea. I stared, and no answer came, because I dared not open my mouth. That day was the beginning of my silence in the face of direct and too-painful grief.

The evening passed. Too hollow for tears, I could not cry. She did not either. My aunt came to stay, to comfort, awkward but kind. She brought me a Mars bar, I don't know why. I went to bed when told, docile, head bowed, wanting to be alone to dissolve in peace without shame.

I felt the first rush and flush of a new grief long to be borne when I opened the bathroom cabinet for toothpaste and in my confusion clutched instead the talc I had given Dad last Christmas. He would never use it again . . . reality slowly crept in like a cold snake and I crawled to bed, the big old double where I had doubtless been conceived. I lay dry-eyed, tears racking my throat, trapped in the layers of inborn reluctance to cry. I knew better than to make a noise and upset Mum; besides, my subconscious added, my guilt held me silent. I cuddled up my knees into my non-existent chest and hugged my guilt to me, nurturing it for future use. It was all I had to remind me of him.

Life was bitter and unwelcome and cruel for me then, and I looked at everything with jaundiced, suspicious eyes. The funeral date was announced, and much fuss was made of the importance of wearing the right garments. Mum was still amazingly dry-eyed – self-protection really, our common trait. I learned it from her by osmosis. Neither of us wanted to unleash the other's suffering, so we stayed locked heavily into our own insecure worlds of guilt, self-blame, punishment and trial. I felt that I had killed him, and knew not if she knew. She, for her part, doubtless felt that their years of mutual alienation were to blame. If only we could have spoken, and broken the spell. But we had neither the courage nor the strength to share our feelings and finally break down. No release-giving Irish wakes in this family now, but a sober ceremony and burial in the nearby cemetery.

It was a bitterly cold day, and we all wore layers of winter wool. Maybe it wasn't the weather, but our view of the proceedings. Mum was collected, in control and bone-tired, you could see that. No tears, and we didn't cling to each other. I kept my head down, and she held hers high. During the service – a Catholic one, a religion my father had despised – the priest tried valiantly to give a good account of Dad, but knew so little about his subject that we all wished desperately that he would end. Eventually the move to the cemetery came and we all trailed outside, Mum's face a study in bitterness and a cold kind of misery.

The reality swept over me, but the funeral itself had seemed to me remarkably false, with the priest's rambling about a man he had never known, and the Mass a ritual of a denomination to which my father did not subscribe.

But I didn't think directly about him or the coffin, and what it must necessarily contain. We stood beside the grave, fresh-dug, as the wind howled dolefully around us. The coffin was lowered into the hole. I averted my eyes. The loneliness of this depth of banishment struck me as my desolate loss did. After the service I was instructed to throw a handful of earth on to the coffin. I couldn't. I felt that would be the final sin, to abandon him frozen to the ground, so I pinched a rose from a nearby family grave and laid that on top instead.

By now we were all blue with cold, my small feet leaden weights. Walking back home, people patted Mum's hand awkwardly and murmured their sympathies, which were received with a bravely regal incline of the head.

Back at the house, my uncle had the hot soup and toddies ready. Believing that we would all need strong alcoholic sustenance – even the two dogs who were present – he had spiked the soup, tea and coffee with generous amounts of brandy. The priest, never a man to refuse a drop of the good stuff, immersed himself in soup. Mum and I could not touch a thing, but wandered from room to room with plates of food; I was amazed that anyone could eat heartily after a funeral. Mum went upstairs to be alone. I curled up on the spare bed and tried very hard not to cry. Somebody's dog ambled drunkenly on to the bed to keep me company, and snored doggy snores. Downstairs, two of the Happy Family were arguing heatedly about politics, both slurry-voiced.

Eventually my cousin came upstairs to see where I was and insisted on my presence downstairs, hissing furiously, 'Why do you always have to be such a drama queen?' Unwillingly, I dragged myself down. My cousin said, 'I found her upstairs sulking. I don't know what's the matter with her.' An older cousin, red-faced and purple-nosed from too much of the soup, rejoined, 'For Christ's sake, what do you think's the matter with her? Her father's just died!'

At this explosive point a distraction occurred – the priest, unused to such overflowing liquid hospitality, had stood in front of the fire to warm himself and had inadvertently set his cassock alight. After much throwing of damp tea-towels and beating-down of flames the man of God slunk home to his stern housekeeper, frantically chewing mints to prevent the smell of brandy from reaching her trained nose.

A farce of a funeral, then; years later, one of my less favourite aunts was to remark on how hilarious this episode was. To those of us sunk deeply into the folds of grief, it was not. After the family had left, each member promising support and kinship, Mum and I were left with each other's company for almost the first time since Dad's death. My uncle had thought it best to leave us in peace for a while; we were to go to them for the weekend, but until then we were at each other's mercy. With no appetite for food, nor desiring sleep, we tried to carry on with our normal pursuits as if nothing had happened. At no time did we acknowledge Dad's death or discuss him and his part in our lives.

I went to school as usual. Mum shopped, cooked, cleaned and went back to work to earn the money for us to live on now that the main source of income was no longer there. The school had been told that my father had died, and that I was to be treated the same as everyone else. The teacher, unnerved by my over-bright eyes and forced smile, took the class aside and told them of my bereavement. My schoolmates dared not mention it to me until I approached the subject of my own accord; this I would not do. I was sure that they did not know, and wanted to keep it that way. The last thing I needed was awkward, artificial curiosity. So we danced a little around each other, they watching me for signs of strain, me full of the effort not to show any. Years later, when we were all a lot more mature, we talked about that period of my life. They had felt rejected, puzzled, that I could not go to them. But we were only kids – and pretty cruel, ruthless kids at that.

Our family policy, now there were only two of us left, was to prevent any unwanted show of sympathy or, far worse, pity from others. One child, not having heard the news, asked me curiously, after a parents' evening when Mum didn't manage to turn up, if I had a Dad and, if so, what did he do? Most of the other children's fathers fell into one of two categories: either they were unemployed or they were professionals – doctors, teachers, solicitors and businessmen. I couldn't seem to slide the real words out. I could not possibly have said, 'He's dead'; that would have brought reality looming dangerously near the horizons of my unreal world, the one that kept me sane. So I stood rooted to the ground, unable to speak, leaving the child to presume that I did not, in fact, have a father; that I was, therefore, a bastard.

The biggest immediate practical worry for Mum and me was lack of money; Dad's firm was to pay us no pension for him, due to some vague illogical technicality. So we learned we would have to scrape by on what my mother earned, plus what little the welfare state was to provide – a meagre widow's pension and a child allowance. We quickly learned to live even more thriftily than we had done before, descending on the local grocer's shop and scouring the shelves for a bargain or two. Before, we had been on the brink of poverty, with a tiny, albeit stable, wage coming in each week. Now, living on the combined force of our wits, poverty occupied the same house as we did. For Mum it must have been a sickening, frightening time, with the fear that she would not be able to earn enough to keep the two of us. But for me it was a novelty and almost an excitement to see how little we could manage on.

I decided to make my own Christmas gifts, and collected soda crystals and dyes to produce home-made bath salts. Mum, catching me dying the crystals a violent, unpalatable blue – and myself and most of the kitchen in the process – hastily assured me that perhaps we didn't have to be quite as innovative as that. Also, she added, she *had* preferred the kitchen in its original colour. We rarely celebrated Christmas anyway. We had when I was very little, and fond aunties and uncles had laden my bedroom with many presents, but as I had grown older the festive season began to hold little appeal for me, and as Mum felt the same we tried not to make too much of a thing of it all. We went down to Mum's sister and brother-in-law usually, but still wished for all the false jollification to be over before it had begun.

Months after Dad's death we were both still deeply

in shock, although I didn't realize it to be that at the time, immersed as we were in our separate but similar unrealities. Firmly ensconced in the vision of life as an assault course, we struggled through, losing touch in a gradual crumble of vagueness and inability to cope on the terms the world insisted on giving us. And, since neither of us could come to terms with the situation we were forced to live with, we coped by opting out and turning to our dreams to block out the pain of reality.

This period of trial and error between Mum and me was not helped greatly by the appearance of a new male figure in our house. Arriving home one day from school I found him sitting in, of all places, my father's chair. It could only have been Dad's, well worn and patched in many places, with cigar ash and strong tea stains, and heavy dips in the arms where Dad had leaned to cheer on the TV wrestlers of a Saturday afternoon from his ringside armchair. The best china was out, and a plate of cake – this, in a household which had not seen luxuries in ages! I was cautious, and barely polite – hardly charming. I wanted to know what he was doing in our house, in That Chair. His name was Frank.

In the course of time I discovered that Frank was the brother of the old lady whom Dad had 'adopted', and that he was nearly eighty; my ridiculous worries about him as a possible replacement Dad were gone. Nobody could want to marry such an old man, I thought disgustedly with the prudish cruelty of callow youth. He was terribly thin, almost skeletal – 'Does nobody feed you?' I asked curiously, to furious glances from Mum's direction. Very tall, he swayed ever so slightly as if his long frame could not balance. He was also very grey all over, as a decaying fish might be, and he smelled as one might do too – a mustiness of ancient and hallowed museum halls. He had a large, apologetic face, loosely wrinkled and jowled, with two great eyes of grey set in cadaverous hollows that regarded my cross, twelve-year-old countenance. He frightened me, and I felt the foundations of my tenuous world shake once more.

Around this time, with our need for money more

important than ever, Mum took a new job in a solicitor's office. Here she took dictation for a blind lawyer, a shaggy man whose ability to use his other senses in replacement for that lost, vital one was strong. One of the partners in the firm, an ex-military man, had the distinctive and unfortunate feature of squeaky shoes – Mum's man would sigh and motion to her to cease scribbling as soon as he heard the noise, knowing that Major Squeaky Boots would be the bearer of doom-laden news.

Do solicitors have any other kind? It was this world of legalities and criminal practice that confirmed my early disillusionment with life. I was an extraordinarily cynical child; I had become so used to trauma, with my parents' ill health and then the breakdown of their relationship, that I thought of it as a normal and expected part of family life. I still felt the guilt of my father's death fresh within me, and was sure that I had caused it. The pain of everyday life I accepted as a necessary evil. Hovering between Catholic prayers and suicidally painful depression, I presumed that this was what everyone's life was like. I was amazed that my contemporaries expected life to be full of the sweetness and joy they constantly encountered. Being Catholic, my ideas were reinforced by such biblical admonitions as: 'All you have is worthless. Give away all but the shirt on your back', 'Be thankful for small mercies because God can take from you any time He chooses to do so', 'Ashes to ashes' – and all *that* jazz.

But I was very slowly beginning, at twelve-going-on-thirteen, to break the spell of Catholicism and discover the truth behind that religion. The trouble was that I had a very large chip of bitterness to weigh my vision down. If God was so all-loving and all-encompassing, how could He have let my Daddy die? Well-meaning relatives tried to tell me, 'Well, dear, he wants to have the good ones with him, doesn't he?' I wasn't having *that*. I felt frustrated in my religious pursuits, surrounded by mad priests who drank too much at a parishioner's funeral and set themselves on fire, and smiled with a frightening, wolf-like intensity.

I bled for the first time, and was taken by surprise

with the heaviness of my periods. I lost enough blood to make me anaemic, and was given iron tablets by the doctor. The bleeding worried me more; I felt that it must be a sin, told as I was that men would smell the blood and come hunting me down. I regarded it as the onset of sexual activity, which of course must only take place within the sanctity of a marriage, and even then only for the procreation of children. Thoughts along lines other than these were a cardinal sin – I felt that guilt must burn me and show me for the harlot I must be to harbour secret thoughts about sex and what It was like, and why It was such an awful, sinful thing to do. I guessed that It must be a very painful and unpleasant thing, and could understand why my parents had slept in separate beds.

It was, therefore, a worrying time when boys began to become creatures to be coy with and to flirt with. The new school I had started in the autumn of the year Dad died was mixed and in a rough area. We girls had to learn a new way of dealing with these creatures who wore aftershave to school and seemed to change the pitch of their voices daily. We did not realize that their adolescent agony was almost certainly worse than ours, as there were few boys compared to the hundreds of females at the school. All of a sudden they wanted to carry our books, give us lifts home on their bikes and buy us Christmas presents – yet at the school discos they would not talk to us, but huddled in a corner in groups, watching us carefully for signals reciprocated.

I found them immature, and looked at the older men in my area for possible beaux. There were several whom I went out with, but having found that their ages belied their maturity, I looked round again, dispirited. I wanted a man to replace the dominant male figure in my life, and I wanted him now. Unfortunately, the man I chose turned out to be far more immature than I, despite the fact that he looked a lot older than his eighteen years.

Alan had recently suffered a loss himself: his father had left the family home for another woman. Feeling very bitter, Alan wanted some sort of awful revenge, but lacked the courage to do anything as brave as tell his father straight what he thought of him. So he seethed in silence. I wanted the whole world to suffer for my father's demise, but my common sense told me that there was no one to blame except myself – and that was where my anger went. So we were well matched in that unfortunate, resentful, frustrated, simmering way, and that is no doubt why the whole relationship was a disaster from beginning to end. I was as mixed up a child-teen as you could find, and he an embittered, fresh-out-of-adolescence, angry young man.

We came together through his persistence; I constantly turned his offers down, and this spurred him on to chase me all the more. I simply wasn't interested. I had already been out with a few unsavoury characters, and I was not ready to start trying to gauge terms of trust and limits of testing each other out with another over-excited boy. But eventually I capitulated, ungracefully.

Alan was physically unlike the lads of my own age: tall and seemingly more self-assured, he was mercifully lacking in adolescent pimples and gauche movements. He took charge on our early dates, ordering the meal, buying the drinks and deciding where we went. He always insisted on paying, and although I had a part-time job I didn't earn enough to pay for the places we went to. He on the other hand was working full-time, and was well paid. The release of responsibility was a welcome one to me. Mum and I were very independent, fiercely so, and here was someone willing to take charge just so long as I dressed up for each occasion and presented the right image. I was unaware of the sacrifices and compromises I would have to make.

After three months of our relationship, obviously a steady one (my friends, abandoned now, couldn't believe that I was seeing someone of eighteen – 'But he's so old . . . '), he told me that he loved me. It was not the most romantic of occasions – we were parked outside the family graveyard. I think Alan decided to resort to the old tell-her-you-love-her-and-she'll-soon-get-them-off trick. I was already convinced that I was unlovable and so I flung him crossly away from me and stormed out of the car.

I felt that it was impossible for me to be loved; if

my own parents could not really love me, why should anyone else? At that time I felt not so much unloved as unregarded; although I was an only child, and was paid a certain amount of attention because of that, my parents had, I believe, seen me at eleven as an adult, who neither needed nor appeared to desire love, or cuddles, or kisses. I suppose I added to the picture by withdrawing into a dream world where everything was always rosy, and by always coping with the various crises that arose. Poor Alan! He was way out of his depth, floundering into such a web of emotional complexities that there was little room for his.

Not long after the episode in the car, I began to stay away from school; among other reasons, I was scared. A lot of bullying went on at this school and the teachers appeared to turn their heads rather than deal with it and get hurt themselves if the bullies had felt so inclined. I wanted desperately to learn and was a keen pupil, always career-minded, who would have welcomed discipline, but my Catholic school had many radical ideas and encouraged us to do whatever we pleased. With no uniform, no set times to be in classes, and often no teacher in the classroom, we learnt nothing except the art of decadence. I was an unattractive child and the other children, being bored, teased me without mercy, finding amusement in my pain. Soon, the taunts and insults became a big enough reason for me not to go to school any more.

So I exchanged the daily stomach-tightening retch of anxiety and fearful anticipation for a mix of boredom and relief, bowels loosening and stomach unknotting a little more as each day I spent away from school passed by. Eyes searching for teachers or truant officers on the prowl, I spent the days wandering around the town, walking on and on, through the hordes of coffee-time shoppers, through the lunchtime office crowds, to the hazy afternoons of midwinter with the sun chilly and sinking early, glad to be gone. Then I flew to the bus, avoiding the accusing eyes of my peers who obeyed the laws of state and attended school every day. Home, in the welcoming warmth, I began a rambling litany of the events of my imaginary day. Depression set into me once more, like mould, and I grew crushed, deadened by the weight of the lies and guilt I had buried myself in. I brooded alone, sitting for hours, thinking, going over and over the day of Dad's final heart attack.

I saw Alan every night and each weekend. I felt as if I were rushing headlong, helpless, inevitable, into something which I would be unable to control. We spoke little, going to loud gigs or noisy pubs where talk was not only unnecessary but impossible. Returning home late at night, he would park outside my house and furtively try to arouse what he supposed was an unawakened passion in me. It was not – it was fear, of God and His retribution, and of Alan himself, whose rough, careless, ignorant hands caused me great pain. I sat in silence filled with resentment at his unspoken assumption that he would be able to have his way with me, sooner or later. I agonized over what to do. Should I go to the priest and confess our progress so far, or should I write to an agony aunt for advice and comfort? The problem was, that I didn't want to have sex with Alan and had no desire for him, but a small part of me felt that I had already committed so many sins that one further one would not make any difference . . . . I was sure that, after causing the death of my own father, I could not sink much lower. In the end, sighing at the folly I knew I was committing, also the sin, I gave in. I let him do whatever he would have described it as. To me it was neither lovemaking, nor sex, but no less than rape with consent. My body was still and acquiescent, but my mind raged against such infiltration. I bled a great deal, painfully, and was sick.

I felt different afterwards, as he silently drove me home. He no doubt felt victorious, whilst I felt justly punished for all my sins. It seemed that my life was always to be drenched in decisions of sin. I chose the wrong path that night, and at thirteen was roughly, painfully, bloodily deflowered. There were no excuses on my part, even though I still blush hotly at writing this. I found it difficult to walk for a week. The shock of the pain enlightened me: so this is why we are all warned away from the horrors of sex. It is not because of fear of pregnancy, but because the pain is too terrible to bear. However, I learnt quickly how to endure the necessary agony. I discovered the sense behind lying back and thinking of England. I composed shopping lists, made up tunes and invented a whole imaginary world of people whilst on my back. Like any old whore, I treated it all as something to be got over with as quickly as possible. In this way did I save my sanity.

Every time, blood still flowed from me. If he noticed, he said nothing, or maybe guilt hit him too. He hurt me and I hated him, silently but steadily. I no longer felt that he was father-like. How could I ever have felt so? I never made any signs of pain, though, but still kept the reserve in place. The awful thing was that I began to see what lay beneath the Catholic doctrines of sex and sin if not accompanied by wedlock. I realized that my only hope of 'keeping my man' lay in the tendrils of sexual entanglement. I began to suspect that he enjoyed hurting me. Maybe, I thought, rationalizing, maybe it was his anger against his father emerging upon the only available outlet — me.

My periods began to suffer from the extraordinary violence; each month brought heavier flows than before, clots of blood betraying the mess inside. I visited a gynaecologist with Mum, terrified that he would carry out some test which would reveal that I was no longer virgo intacta. He did not, but without a full examination, he said, he could not discern the cause of the trouble. I of course could not tell him or Mum what I thought was causing the monthly eruptions. I reiterated to myself that this was what I deserved, so I must suffer. Alan and I continued in this way, both silent with our real feelings. I reached a pitch of depression and guilt so painful that it hurt me like a pain, a tension, in my chest. By now I was also agoraphobic, and found it really difficult to go outside. I had started to have a real fear of men, and would flinch if one looked at me. I was convinced that every man who walked behind me was about to rape me: my palms would grow sweaty, my hands trembling, my walk faster and faster. Eating out became a nightmare. Alan, in an attempt to hide his own ill-ease, took to teasing me about the genteel way I ate until I could not eat or drink in public for fear of everyone in the restaurant turning to look at me and dissolving into laughter. The improbability of this never occurred to me.

I spent all my spare time with Alan, partly because I was afraid he would leave me, and partly because Frank's presence in our house made me feel like some sort of a gooseberry. So my friends saw little of me, and I of them. They would have shied away from the subject of my sexual dilemma and I felt uncomfortable, unclean, in their presence.

I started to plan, quite deliberately, my exit from this world of coldness and misery. Mum always had pills in the house – some for her insomnia, some for other mysterious reasons. There were also packets of aspirin for the headaches we both suffered from almost constantly. I had considered drowning: too risky – some well-meaning person would undoubtedly come to my aid. Throwing myself in front of a bus: it was always possible that the bus would be able to stop in time. (In later years, I found out that one of my distant relatives had tried this method. The man had lain prone in the middle of a crossroads expecting the bus to go over him at full speed; instead, the driver had turned left, leaving the unfortunate man looking remarkably foolish in the middle of the road, while amused pedestrians looked on.) No, the only ways open to me, I decided, were overdosing or wrist-slashing. I was able to be very calculating about all this. It seemed to me, at the time, to be simply something I had to do, a necessary evil like having sex or going to Mass or going to confession. It all had to be very orderly, even civilized.

I opted for two bottles of Paracetamol and crept, fearful, into my tiny bedroom. I took all I could swallow without retching, sure that I had taken enough to see the end of me. I lay down, feeling curious, waiting for a violent reaction. I dozed off undramatically after a while. Mum must have come home, seen the empty bottles and panicked – she rang the hospital, who sent an ambulance round and hoisted me, prone, on to a stretcher. White-faced and hollow-eyed, Mum sat stiffly beside me, too buttoned-up with contained anger to speak. Shame and guilt settled in beside me and I lay back woozily, a little sluggish but most definitely not a suicidal success. I knew now the real meaning of despair – the inability to take even your own life.

Arriving at the hospital, I smelled the disinfectant of the corridors through which I had walked to my fathers' death-bed. Wheeled into the casualty department, white silence in a clinical night, I was told to strip and lie down on the green-papered bed. Stern-faced nurses told me I had to stay very still and open my mouth wide. They were going to 'pump me out', and they said they were going to be rough with me and make the experience so unpleasant that I wouldn't repeat the attempt. They took their time, deliberately. My throat, already dry with nervous anticipation, contracted when I caught sight of the huge, boa constrictor-sized tube they intended to force downwards into my raging, turbulent stomach. The doctor, a thin young man with bloodshot eyes and a nervous rash of angry pimples, peered myopically at me and declared that the time was right for the tube to descend. I was warned by a brisk, Führer-like nurse that if I did not comply I would have the tube forced up my nose. 'One way or another, we'll get that stuff out of you,' she said. Alarmed, I swallowed hastily.

It was the most painful experience to have while still fully conscious – warm curls of fluid and bile flew up the tube and on to the nurses' uniforms. Tutting, with venomous glances at me, they continued their work with renewed vigour. After two hours of this thoroughly awful punishment I was taken, weak, exhausted and almost crying with pain, to the ward for an overnight stay.

I awoke early, as one does in hospital, in a ward full of teenagers with broken limbs. I could not swallow, and for a change could barely croak any words. I waved away the morning coffee and was told that the doctor would see me on his ward round. He strode over accompanied by the usual gaggle of students, and peered at my white face. 'She'll live,' he announced – glumly, I thought. He sounded disappointed; but not as disappointed as I was. The next visitor was the hospital psychiatrist, a brusque red Scot with ill-matching ginger hair plentiful upon his head. He fingered his beard and studied me with his pale, gooseberry eyes, looking like a man who had just discovered a new species. He announced that I was to see him every week, as if wasn't I the lucky girl now?

On the bus home, I reflected upon it all. Had anything been achieved? I guessed not. Mum's chief worry had been that the neighbours would find out what all the 'fuss' had been about. All I really felt was a terrible anti-climax, the staleness of which was a bitter aftertaste to what I had hoped would be a quick passage to death, but instead had turned out to be a sore throat and an unknown quantity to be faced back at home.

Looming large in the depression I felt soaking through me was a heap of regrets over our rapidly deteriorating relationship. Mum and I were blood-close in an unbreakable, uncomfortable bond of like-repels-like, but our daily life was fraught with so many areas of no-go on either side. There were no arguments about what time I must be in, or about unsuitable boyfriends, or heavy make-up; our life was lived as carefully as walking on a minefield of Subjects That Must Not Be Mentioned. Included amongst these were sex, my reluctance for religion, my father, his death . . . .

It was truly now as though Dad had never existed. No photographs, no memories at all. I felt I knew nothing about him, about his likes or dislikes, his habits, his hobbies, his desires, his frustrations. Mum was closed to me. I walked through never-ending rain to his grave, an unmarked one with no headstone at that time, a sombre patch of soil with dying encrusted flowers. I bought the roses he loved, Peace, a golden-peachy variety, and placed them on the grave, my tears crystallizing in the rain. I downed the umbrella and walked home, letting the raindrops soak me. Dad too had liked the rain. One day, angry at my pilgrimage to his grave, Mum had greeted me on my return with: 'I wish you had never been born. You are a freak, do you know? A freak. You have a heart only of stone.' I felt this to be true. I felt there was no heart beating in me, only much pain, and sorrow, and the everlasting guilt. I would sit cuddling my few memories of him to me – the smell of the linseed oil he used to clean his paintbrushes with, the golden sunflowers he magicked on to paper as I sat, a child, entranced – this was the nearest I ever got to releasing my grief, still pinned tightly inside me.

Since my suicide attempt, nothing had changed in our little world. I grew restless again. Alan was irritated with my wildly swinging moods. I looked around once more for a way to escape this unbearable monotony of depression, tension and hidden grief. In the bathroom my eye fell upon a pack of razor blades, and my mind registered them as a potential suicide tool. This time, I was quite determined that nothing should go wrong. I went out into the night and bought two tubes of Paracetamol. On my return I took them all, swallowing them down with gin. Unpacking the blades, I tested one on my finger: not very sharp, but they would work, surely? Drawing one across my left wrist, I found it much more difficult to hurt myself than I had imagined. The warm blood was sickening, and my heart thudded uncomfortably in a sort of repulsion. Again and again I pulled the rusty blade over my now raw skin, but I could not seem to go very deep. Sawing away, I began to feel weaker. Soon I could not see properly, and could not walk at all. The combination of alcohol and tablets must have started to work.

Once again I passed into semi-consciousness, and was interrupted by Mum's return from the shops, coming upstairs to put away her coat. She must have seen the trail of blood from the bathroom to the bedroom and came running in to see me – outstretched on the bed, unable to focus on anything, with dripping wrists. She summoned the ambulance once more. And so it all began again. Soon I arrived back at the same hospital, with the sickness of anticipated treatment – the nurses were different, the doctor an older man, but the pain was as bad. Down went the tube. Up came the poison. Swiftly my sore wrists, like rare steaks, were bandaged and I was wheeled to the ward to rest for the night. Waking early again the next morning, I waited for the inevitable crowd of doctors, students and psychiatrists . . . .

It was the same shrink, confident in his 'I told you so' mouthed to my mother. He was aware, he said, that teenage girls tried this sort of thing to gain attention they felt they were lacking. We felt a mutual dislike for each other, but were obliged to meet weekly. He passed my case on to his assistant, not wanting the task of trying to persuade me that he was right in his diagnosis and I was wrong. The assistant was a pleasant woman who smiled helplessly and was unable to answer any of my questions, fielding them all with, 'Well, we'll have to ask Dr McTurk about that, won't we?' He himself was never there. I decided that these fruitless visits were a waste of my time, and so I stopped going.

During this time of excessive upheaval my mother's only friend, old Frank, with whom she had spent most of her time, died. Mum had been acting as a sort of unpaid housekeeper. Their relationship was a complex one: Frank, a lonely widower himself, had delighted in giving my mother expensive furs and jewellery that had belonged to his late wife; Mum's thirst for the best had not diminished with the years of poverty. Although they would probably have raised quite a bit of money had she sold them, she would never have considered it while Frank was alive; they were gifts from his dead wife's collection, and to be given them was a great honour. You do not sell things like that. He took her to the best restaurants in the area and was adept at paying her regular compliments, conscious of how she feared the onset of age. Aware of our financial difficulties, he left his entire estate to Mum, to the surprise of his remaining relatives. We were released from our jail of poverty then – and the first item Mum spent her money on was my education. At fifteen I was whisked away from the Catholic radical school and planted in a private girls' school for the remaining nine months of my education. The class I joined consisted of five other girls, by whom I was instantly outcast because, as one of them put it, 'You don't have a swimming pool or even a car!' Their parents were all nouveau-fairly-rich, and they looked down their noses at me. I was therefore fairly isolated within the new school, but at least the old-fashioned teaching methods gave me an incentive to work for my impending O-levels. I was eager to learn, but was ignorant of many of the basic facts and essentials such as essays and précis. I had only nine months until my O-levels and I was determined to get some results. The teachers threw up their hands in horror at my ignorance, but agreed grudgingly that like clay, I might be shaped into something promising.

I felt as if my life was at last gradually dividing into two parts – a settling down at school for the first time, and a turbulent sea in which Alan, Mum and I floated uneasily, narrowly avoiding black rocks and clinging to every small buoy of comfort. We were living in a sense of stalemate, an uneasy, truce-like situation. The relationship between Alan and me continued to exist, for devious reasons of our own, while my once-idealistic expectations of love floundered and died. Mum and I were as content in our enforced togetherness as either of us could expect to be, while I stayed in a relationship she could not approve of. She did not know about my sexual awakening, but was wary of the seeming steaminess and long-term possibilities of our 'romance'.

I blossomed a little in confidence at the new school and made some friends, though not without enduring a testing phase of half-hearted bullying, a kind of initiation. My schoolwork improved by huge leaps, and I learnt the pure joy of reading Shakespeare, Lawrence, Hardy and Dickens in a disciplined and essay-related way. My career plans were beginning to take vague but eventual shape. I decided that I would definitely write for a living, as I had previously thought, and draw as well, and the time that I had previously devoted to following Alan around like a lost sheep began to be used productively in planning my way to fame or riches. I read voraciously, as before, and wrote stories that won local competitions. I felt truly at home with Tolstoy's Anna Karenina or Hardy's Tess, living in a fantasy daydream of the world of my tragic heroines; and I loved to be chilled and chastened by Kafka and Günter Grass, feeling less of an oddity when I was immersed in *The Trial* and the nightmare world of *Cat and Mouse*. This appreciation of good literature, originally encouraged at home by my mother, had continued at my previous school. There I had taken refuge from the bullying hordes in the library and feasted on the treasures I found therein. My contemporaries eyed my school bag, suspicious because I read such weighty tomes while they fingered the pages of Jackie Collins et al.

During this year of preparations for my future, 1984, I fell into a sudden lethargic depression from which nothing could rouse me. It happened at the worst possible time. I cared for nothing, dragged myself to school only because I dared not play truant (in a class of six, one missing was noticeable), and cried listlessly though still silently throughout the night. I knew not where the depression had come from, or how to banish it; consequently I passed only four out of nine exams – a small feat for one who had not revised.

Alan joined the army that year and was posted to Germany after a brief period of training in England. I saw very little of him, but did not care. I wanted to end the relationship but the coward within me persuaded me that it wasn't worth breaking it up – after all, I would only see him once or twice a year. The truth was, my self-esteem was so low that I was firmly convinced that no other man would want me. So I stayed with him, and braced myself for each fresh onslaught upon my body.

Mum and I were at the stage of cautious negotiations about our future. She was tired of life in Kenilworth, having lived there all her life, and for several months had been toying with the idea of moving right away from the area and escaping the eyes of those who had known her from years back. Our house had no fond memories of Dad for her, only a reminder that her social progress had been effectively frozen. Now that I was between O-levels and A-levels she had a chance to leave all her past behind and move into other pastures, green or otherwise. The question was, where to go? It was a bit like closing your eyes and sticking a pin on a map at random. Mum's sister and her husband lived in Northamptonshire and we had visited them a couple of times; quiet and countrified, it seemed as suitable as anywhere. We found a bungalow in a town called Brackley, which is where we went to live. I was a little bewildered, but acquiesced – what choice did I have? I certainly had no regrets about leaving Kenilworth, and even felt stirrings of optimism about the idea of a fresh start in a new town. I could make new friends who knew nothing of my rather strange past, and attend a new school where I could wipe clean the slate and start A-levels, to cover the dimness of my O-level failure with shining glory. Here was my chance to erase the memories of the past, and the mistakes too.

Chapter Four

We arrived in Brackley on a sunless day in the middle of June 1984. For a Saturday afternoon the town seemed remarkably quiet. A large, ugly town hall dominated the market square. We noticed some peculiarly quaint shops – a violin maker, a riding tackle shop, an old-fashioned tailor. There were a couple of dilapidated old pubs, and a tree-lined avenue closeting the old school-house, now a boarding place for sixth-form pupils. It felt cold and windy, full of empty spaces. No cars cluttered the car park; there were few shoppers. No one browsed. I was not impressed, but remembered that my attempt must be to Think Positive. Before unloading our personal bits and pieces, we stopped for lunch at the largest of the pubs: timbers crumbling with authenticity, rounded country accents, dusty grey gloom inside. We were regarded with lively curiosity by the locals, who observed us openly and with delighted amusement at our 'towniness'.

Approaching our new bungalow, I fell silent. It was on an estate, newly built, full of little houses that seemed to me to be all exactly the same – nothing but houses stretched to the skyline either way, and bulldozers on the horizon were paving the way for more monstrosities to be built to house the needy.

None of this I voiced to Mum; she was in an anxious state already, with the whole process of moving house. It had not been easy, but her experience of coping alone had begun immediately after Dad's death, when she had refused all offers of help to organize the funeral details and the business with the will that followed. Now she was exhausted, and wanted only to rest before tackling the huge wooden packing cases that waited in the bedroom, where they had been put on arrival.

The first few days in our new home were full of activity, which kept both of us from brooding as to whether we had done the 'right thing'. It was too early to tell, and we were both inclined to be fatalistic about a decision as soon as we had made it. We unpacked and settled in, sorted out and threw out, called in painters and decorators to attend to the house, and tried to make the best of what we had now got. I ran out to explore the area, strange and new to me. I had expected the Northamptonshire countryside to be beautiful – instead it was flat and bleak and unwelcoming, like the inhabitants of the town.

I was determined to get a part-time job and I also intended to infiltrate myself into the world of journalism in some vague, as yet undefined way. Meanwhile, I had to think about the more imminent matter of starting at the nearby sixth-form college. With my disastrous track record of truancy, and the problems I had had with bullying and alienation, I was nervous at the thought of starting at yet another place of education. I wanted so badly to make friends, to have a normal sixteen-year-old's life and to mix with people of my own age.

Alan and I had been to clubs, fairly expensive ones, restaurants and bars, and I guessed that the Brackley teenagers would have a vastly different social scene. I was right – on my first day at the college I saw notices proclaiming 'Disco! In Common Room, 6.30 – 10p.m.'. No one seemed at all friendly at first, and I began to feel dispirited. I soon learned why I got no response to my overtures – in an aside heard in that eternally useful fount of overheard information, the ladies' lav. I was an outsider. It wasn't just that I was new to the school: it was the way I spoke, my voice distinctly lacking the soft, Northamptonshire burr, and the way I dressed, at odds with my blue-jeaned, anoraked fellow pupils. At the end of that first day my face was stiff from constantly smiling at people, hoping in vain for a response. They all looked very suspicious and grouped together, watching me. At four o'clock I trooped home, too miserable to notice the beautiful sunset over the big hill, halfway down which stood our little bungalow.

In the weeks that followed, I began to worm my way into the ranks of my contemporaries; they thought of me as 'weird', but grew to accept me. I had sneaked into the requirements for taking A-levels by telling a few white ones; I had indicated, without actually lying, that I had the necessary O-levels for the subjects I wanted to take: Art, French and English Literature. I was a little out of my depth in the French, perhaps due partly to the terrifyingly Boadicea-like teacher, who had a sharp tongue and an even sharper eye for a nervous linguist. I hastily changed from French to art history before I could be discovered for the fraud I was. There was no teacher for this subject, but I worried not, certain that I could tutor myself; it held a fascination for me, and I followed my own schedule of art-through-the-ages with a passion. The English classes too I loved, revelling in the books I had already learned to enjoy.

Soon I had found myself the part-time job I wanted, in a local video rental shop. I was working five nights a week, and earning enough to keep myself in clothes and little luxuries for Mum. Surprisingly, for I knew no one, I was happy there, once I learned to overcome my blushes at the remarks of the American soldiers from the nearby base, who comprised the majority of the customers.

So there I was, making some headway at last, with a job to earn me some money, a few friends at college, and an unblotted copybook. It was not to last long. But for the meantime I capitalized upon my new-found normality, feeling even so that it was a guise which might at any moment slip and reveal the real me.

My friends were the other outcasts, one a girl whose parents had left her to live in the boarding house, the second a girl from another town who was as alien as I, and the third a girl who was part of the local crowd, but very eccentric. She was, I thought (perhaps jealously), unnaturally close to her father, and her relationship with him left her on the suspicious side of the other children's comments. We four joined forces. I had accepted by now that I would never fit in with the majority of people, and I refused to sacrifice my individuality simply to fit in with the expected idea of how a sixteen-year-old should be. My new friends would have baulked in horror had they known the details of my life – my sex life with Alan, my attempts to commit suicide, my depressions. In a small, conventional town like Brackley I wasn't prepared to become a total outcast by revealing these secrets – so I compromised. I dressed flamboyantly, and spouted ambitious ideas, but kept my other opinions and peculiarities to myself, remembering that a new start meant discarding the old attitudes.

So, in my new guise of convention, I was as happy as I expected to be. My job enabled me to indulge my major weakness, clothes – I was, without doubt, a clothesaholic. I would trip off to the nearest shopping centre and return hours later, laden down with bags of garments, costume jewellery and accessories. The pity was that I never went anywhere to wear them, so the only place they adorned was the inside of my wardrobe.

Mum and I went to church as regularly as before. She herself went two or three times a week – partly, I suppose, to fill up her days. What else had she to do? The nearest town of any interest was Banbury, ten miles away, or Oxford, twenty; she did not drive, and there were only two buses a day. The Brackley Catholics, liking to know everything about strangers in their midst, were brazen enough to stop Mum outside the church and enquire where her husband was. She would smile distantly and turn the conversation, deftly, to the weather, or the priest's interminably boring sermon. He was an ancient man, wrinkled and musty as such worthies often are, and fond of both a tipple and a smoke. Consequently, he often forgot what he was saying, and never a sermon was given without a timely interruption from one of his brethren, reminding him where he had got to.

The antics of the country ladies who ran the church never failed to amuse me. The priest did not stand a chance against these wiry pensioners: Mapp and Lucia would have quailed at them. One, a stout, purple-haired creature, built like the figurehead on a ship, used to be accompanied by her husband, a sycophantic man who would always doze off halfway through the sermon and would receive a loud hiss-and-curse to awaken him. This same lady once accosted Mum on the church steps and insisted that she help in their religious endeavours; within a few minutes, my mother was assigned to be chief flower-arranger. It was their little world, these stalwart people, and they ran a tight ship.

I did not exactly feel as if I was yet a part of Brackley; the other kids I met were, to my way of thinking, peculiar. They had no ambition, no overt desires for a career or even a job. There was no unemployment problem as such in the town, but their attitude seemed to be one of sloth, and reluctance to take a job which would only pay a few pounds more than the dole. I recoiled in horror at the thought of being dependent upon such a bizarre system as the DHSS, and worked in a variety of jobs in Brackley to ensure that I was never in that position. The idea of waiting until you left university, then just presuming that jobs would be available, filled me with amazement. I was not sure that I would ever be so lucky as to get a place when the time came, and anxiously paved the way with standby alternatives.

In my second term I spoke at length to a careers officer who came to see us all. He told me, after listening to my diatribes, that it would be impossible for me to get into journalism or any related media field without a degree. This he had divined from reading NUJ leaflets of *circa* 1979. I felt that my potential for good A-level results was low, partly because for two of my three subjects I had no teacher (there was only me in the class that year and one pupil did not warrant a tutor). So I taught myself and though I knew I had ability I did not know if I was learning in the right way. My chances of a university place were nil. After this interview I went home and phoned the local newspaper, wanting to know what my chances of writing for them were. At the offices I was told by a brisk but kindly deputy editor that, yes, they took on trainee reporters at eighteen with English

A-level. I fixed up a week of work experience with them and trotted home, satisfied that I was to have a chance to test myself as a writer.

It was at this time that I began to look around me and see that all the other girls had boyfriends of their own age, who shared their interests. I was still seeing Alan, but he was in Germany and came home only once or twice a year. There were plenty of youngish American soldiers in the area, and I began going out with one of them. It wasn't too long before I found out he was married, but he was very philosophical about this. 'Well, she's just had a baby, and she doesn't seem interested in me any more,' he said, shrugging, holding out his hands as if to say: 'This is the way of the world.' It wasn't the way of *my* world, though. I shrugged him off, and looked around again.

There was a feeling in the town that if you didn't have a boyfriend there was something wrong with you. If, on the other hand, you had too many boyfriends, there was something else wrong with you – only something much worse of course. You were a Hussy, a girl who was Not Very Nice, someone of Low Morals. I so desperately wanted to be thought of as normal, and not to stand out in any way, that in a mad effort to please I veered from self-consciously stating that I had a boyfriend away in the army to seeing several different men in the space of a fortnight – all in an attempt to find the Right One. Sometimes these forays were innocent, sometimes not. None of them was at all pleasurable for me, but that I had learned to expect.

I was not happy in this degrading and desperate search for male company, and when Alan came home on his infrequent trips I clung to him and wished for some kind of solace, I knew not what. Maybe the traditional values and expectations of the town were starting to get to me – the push towards marriage, motherhood, 'settling down'. The more I wanted to succumb to this, the more it seemed like cowardice to give in and take the easy path instead of sticking out for what I wanted – a career, independence, fulfilment. I was not so sure if I would ever marry, produce children and have a normal, conventional relationship. During my week at the local paper I discovered that I had the ability to write copy and to form features. I was not a brilliant writer, but I knew how to capitalize on my small skill, and not long afterwards I was writing regular articles for three local papers. For me, this was an achievement: it gave me some confidence to see my work in print, and to know that I might possibly get a job on a paper without a degree.

That was the summer of 1985, and on all counts it looked to be a good one. But I had started lately to have headaches again, which I had suffered continually as a child, together with bouts of lethargy and slight depression. I tried to shake it off, and to comprehend why, when I was trying to assemble my life into a reasonable shape, the black depression should strike once more. I was now on holiday from college for the customary six weeks, and I felt there was no reason to get up in the morning. I gave up my job in the video shop. I wanted to cry all the time, for no apparent cause, and felt that life held nothing for me. I was lonely – Mum and I got along with each other warily, cautiously, but she had never been able to show emotion or express love, let alone kiss or hug. I felt a desperate need for some kind of relationship in which the love that I had to give would be accepted, without conditions or rejection. Waves of the old feelings washed over me – the suicidal wishes, the darkness, the utter, unending sleeplessness. Mock A-levels were imminent on my return to school. But nothing mattered.

One morning I went to the local doctor, a kindly but distant man. After I had explained my predicament he told me that it was not really a matter to come to a GP about, insinuating that I was taking up his time unnecessarily because I was still suffering from the effects of adolescence. That, he informed me, was the reason for my depression, my insomnia, my lethargy. I told him something of my psychiatric history and asked if maybe I could see a psychiatrist. He replied firmly that the diagnosis would be just the same as his was. There was nothing for it, he intoned, except time, and I would then grow out of it. His parting shot was that I was to 'come back in a month or two if you're not feeling any better, dear'.

A month was too long to wait. But in any case I seriously doubted if a psychiatrist could have done anything to help me, since I needed no help in analysing what my problem was; what I needed was a solution. I had come to admit to myself that the driving, dominant need in me was to have something of my own, someone who needed me and loved me, and would not easily reject me. It was a little while before the obvious solution came to me: a baby! Of course. A child who would love me, see no wrong in me, not criticize me, a child whom I could lavish love and affection upon, and cuddle and kiss, and watch grow.

All the time I had been sleeping with Alan, I had left the burden of contraception to him; this was because I have such a forgetful and absent-minded nature that I know I would never remember to take the Pill regularly, and in truth I was afraid that, if I went to the doctor for contraception, he would have told my mother. Or perhaps I just wanted to evade the responsibility I would have to take if 'something went wrong'. So all I had to do when I next saw Alan was to assure him that I had changed my mind about the Pill. This he would not be able to check up on, and so with luck I would conceive. At no point did I intend to tell Alan of my pregnancy, or involve him in any way at all. I wanted this to be *my* baby.

The peculiar thing was that in all these machinations I never considered the time beyond the conception – I had blocked out the reality of the nine months to be endured, then the labour, the resulting child and its needs. All I could see stretching ahead of me was the blatant need, *hunger*, for love, and for someone to need *me* . . . love was all, and I had come to a point of no return as far as emotion was concerned. I knew with utter certainty that if I did not act now I would lose the will to live.

Alan came back to me in July of 1985 for a week, before going back on duty, unaware of how his body was to be used. I endured the pain of sex joyfully, willing the process of growth to begin. At last I had a purpose, a driving force and a need to live. Slowly the depression lifted, as I knew it would with the promise of a new life to salve the old pain of unburdened grief. I felt that this was to be the New Year of my life, the turning point. It must be a boy – no girls to be a pattern of myself, but a boy, brave and handsome, brilliant, a star, the creature I would live for. Reality stayed on the doorstep still and came no further in.

I waited until my period was due, each day an interminable time of hoping and wanting. There was no sign of blood. I felt conviction that at last something good and sweet had been wrenched from all the bad years. Soon it was September, and I knew without any possible doubt, all through my body, that I was pregnant. A peace descended upon me.

But at the same time nausea struck me. I took to missing morning lectures, in fear of rushing out to throw up the acidic bile that was the result of much retching. Back pains assailed me and I ached all through my school day, twisting and turning on the hard, unkind chairs. The others regarded me with curiosity, but probably put these strange squirmings down to the fact that I couldn't be expected to behave as they did because I was unfathomably, unreasonably 'different'. I did my mock A-levels without a backward glance or a spot of revision, and scraped by, warned by my teachers that I would have to pull up my socks and other things if I wanted to pass the real exams in the summer. What did I care for such things? I had a new life to think about, a second little person to account for.

I had taken on another part-time job, and was working hard to get some money together. But I had no time to think about other practicalities. I had seen no doctors, made no hospital visits. No one else knew, and I hugged the secret of my own making close to me, loving what I had so newly created. I felt that it was all my own work. Alan's part being only incidental, an accident of fate.

By December, I was approximately five and a half months pregnant. Up to this point my belly had hardly risen – due to my paranoia about anyone guessing I constantly held my stomach in with great effort, and had to be very careful about the way I composed myself when sitting. All this was made easier because Alan was away from home again, having made a flying visit in November when my belly was innocently flat: he was not to return until April. But I was now feeling so-called 'morning sickness' all day long, and I also had that awful inability to control the bladder that comes with pregnancy. There was also the little question of periods – I decided that it might be wiser to have one every now and again in case Mum became too suspicious. I bought sanitary towels as usual and disposed of them down the loo.

At Christmas we were invited to some relatives for the festive season, and my uncle remarked at the weight I had put on. I bit back the obvious retort and sat silent. Mum noticed nothing. With the New Year I began to think about going to a doctor. I was six and a half months pregnant before I eventually went. My stomach was still flattish, and the hapless GP assumed me to be about two months gone. Ever ready to believe something which I knew could not possibly be true, I announced in a swift and unexplained change of direction that I wanted an abortion. He sighed heavily, and enquired gingerly about my contraception. I was silent, feeling the unspoken disapproval of the doctor. The sensible and little-heard me thought of the advanced state of my condition. The other, wildly scared, woken-up me demanded that the unborn be wrenched out of me. I felt no love for it, no feeling of belonging, but instead fear, anguish and premonition.

The doctor, unaware of all this turbulence, despatched me to the obstetrician in Oxford. This man did not take appearances for granted and sent me off to the scanner; I was returned to his office to be told that I was over twenty-seven weeks pregnant, and what was my GP thinking of to be telling me that I could have an abortion? Ever the coward, I omitted to tell him that I had not been completely honest with the GP. I slunk back to Brackley in a whirlpool of indecision, fear and anger at my own stupidity. The unreality had become real. I had not, indeed, thought beyond conception. In my desperate search for something to love I had failed to envisage the meaning of pregnancy and the responsibility of motherhood.

Home, encased in misery and reality, I turned savagely

to thoughts of removal of the foetus. Thinking of the baby inside me as 'it', I rang joylessly around all the abortion clinics, trying to find one that would take me in, no questions asked, never mind the legal ruling on maximum age of foetus. I found one eventually, a seedy-sounding place in Brixton, who assured me that I would not have to have a scan and that their fees were £400. I did not have the money, and in the end I knew that I had not the courage (or the cowardice?) to go through the trauma of having a child ripped cruelly out of me – a child who had not asked to be born, and whose welfare I had thought nothing of.

There was nothing left but to have the wretched child, and try to find a way to hide it all from Mum. God knows, I knew not how I would accomplish this, but I had to try. I had known all along that to find out that I had been engaged in a sexual relationship, let alone having an illegitimate baby, would kill her. I had been guilty of too much sorrow in the past to want to incur more now. So, sitting there telephone in hand, I made the decision to find a suitably discreet way of having the child, then to deal with the problem of adoption or whatever the alternatives were.

I went to the local social services office, where I was assigned to a particularly odious social worker whom I would not have liked under any circumstances, but who seemed especially horrid and lacking in diplomacy to one who needed help on adoption. She was too old for the job, and I disliked her patronizing attitude. She treated me like a naughty little girl who had foolishly and selfishly got herself pregnant, and rubbed in the harshness of her views by insisting on our interviews taking place in an office bright with children's toys and posters full of happy parents. Rubbing my immorality in, perhaps? They had no right to, especially as the story I told her was a virtuous one – if untrue.

As far as they knew I was a rape victim, and my soon-to-be-born child was the result. I had concocted this story in order to save me from their relentless prying about the father, and to save Alan from any involvement with the paternity of a baby he knew nothing about and had been unwittingly duped into fathering. I alleged that I had been going into Oxford to meet a friend, and had missed her (this part was true). There had been no buses back to Brackley, so I had gone to the station. From the timetable I had seen that I could get direct to Weston-super-Mare, and had thought, on impulse, to go there and try to rekindle some of the happiness I had experienced there as a child (this part also was true). I had arrived at Weston at midnight. I had had no money to go to a hotel, so walked along the beach, where, to cut a long lie short, I was raped. It was the kind of story that no one could actually disprove – they were, I'm sure, very sceptical, but they could not prove that I was lying.

It was a dreadful lie to tell, and a dreadful subject to lie about, but I really didn't see why Alan should be involved in any adoption proceedings, especially since I hadn't even let him know I was pregnant. I hadn't seen him since July and he was due home in March, one month before I was due to give birth. I had tried to put him off seeing me, because I didn't want to have to face him with the obvious statement of my big belly and tell him either the awful, cringe-making lie or the even more crass truth.

This was a minor consideration besides all the machinations I had to work out to cover up the period of delivery. I knew of a dreadfully dismal-sounding home for 'girls like me' which I thought would be better than nothing, but to my surprise it was full up. Too many unmarried mothers in Northampton. However, by a piece of miraculous luck the woman in charge of the hostel offered me a room in her house while I was having the baby; I jumped at the offer.

Then I turned to the question of how I was going to explain my necessary absence from home. It occurred to me that I would tell Mum I had been offered a place on a journalism course in London. I had had to tell her so many lies about days out at college interviews lately that one more made no odds. I had had 'interviews' in the last few months in Liverpool, Cardiff, Birmingham and many other places while I had actually been at the hospital or the hateful social services offices.

I had not seen much of Mum lately, even though I had been off school and at home quite a lot of the time. Some days I wanted to tell her so badly, and only just stopped myself in time. It would have been such a selfish thing to do, but I felt as though the combination of the pressure of the baby, and the A-levels, and my jobs, and the thoughts of the future, would crush me.

When I told her about the course she was not even sceptical. This worried me – usually she mistrusted everything I said, with good reason, but now she seemed to be absent-mindedly accepting without question. I had been trying for a long time to persuade her to do a job, or take up voluntary work, to get her out of the house and interested in something; but since the move to Brackley she had got more and more bitter, resenting the town and its inhabitants, the simple rural ways and the lack of public transport. Feeling herself trapped, she even talked of going back to Kenilworth and started ordering the Kenilworth and Coventry papers and sending for house details from estate agents there.

It was now the end of March, and I was getting nervous, imagining what might happen if I were to give birth ridiculously early or late. There was a limit to what Mum would believe. Alan was home for the first time since November and he was determined to see me. In due course he called round and took me to a nearby town for a drink, where I sat nervously in the pub while I tried to think of ways of broaching the subject if I had to tell him. I was intending to tell *him* the rape story too, knowing that he would willingly accept a load of lies rather than have to take on a responsibility. In any case, I didn't expect him to take any responsibility for something that he had, in all fairness, been unaware of.

After leaving the pub we drove to my home. We sat in silence outside the little bungalow until finally he turned to me with a sigh and said, 'Why don't you just tell me what's the matter?' Taking a deep, shaky breath, I did so. He sat in silence until I had finished my recital of lies, and then I waited for his reaction. It was as much of an anti-climax as it could be. He looked embarrassed, cleared his throat and asked me, uncomfortably, what I wanted him to do. I looked at him, amazed. 'I don't want *you* to do anything.'

I added a postscript to the story, to the effect that I was simply telling him about it before he found out for himself, and that I wanted nothing from him, financially, emotionally or otherwise. That, I said, had been my reason for not wanting to see him, and I would quite understand if he wanted to spend his leave doing other things. But he said he would still see me, and only had a few days' leave before going out to Northern Ireland on duty.

Alan was obviously taken aback by the news, although relieved to hear that he was expected to play no part in the birth. I had told him I would take care of everything, and that he was to forget all about it. When he came home again, it would all be over. We spent the remaining few days together.

I was to go to the social worker's house on 1 April, the same day that Alan was due to go to Ireland. I had had a lot of difficulty with Mum over her insistence that this hostel I would be staying in, in London, must surely have a telephone number and an address. I managed to persuade her eventually that I would ring her, and so she insisted on giving me some money to take with me for 'phone calls from London' and other expenses. I was reluctant to take it, but in a bid to seem unsuspicious I did. Then I packed, taking plenty of books for the weeks which I knew would be filled with waiting. I felt that I really should take some revision, but had no enthusiasm and knew that these days my mind was too far away to contemplate reading Shakespeare and Milton.

Arriving at the bus station in Northampton where I was to meet Mrs Farrell, I lugged my heavy case round and felt winded. I was really conscious of my stomach now, although it still hardly showed, and I had constant backache because I had never been able to be visibly pregnant at home or anywhere else, and had to be very careful of sitting in a way that, although comfortable, might display my shape. I had no idea that I should have been taking iron supplements, especially as I had a history of anaemia; I had not been eating properly, and rarely drank milk. I had carried on with my three jobs and my studies and my writing, and had carried and lifted heavy objects without thought for the unborn child.

I had to register at a different hospital because I was moving over the county border, so I made an appointment. It was a Friday when I arrived at Mrs Farrell's house. It was out in an isolated part of the countryside, too far to walk to the nearest village, and ten miles from the town where the hospital was. I dreaded the thought of the drive there, down a rocky, uneven lane, when I would be in labour. Maybe I would be in too much pain to notice, though.

I spent the weekend in the most miserable state of depression I had ever encountered. I was bored, and felt uncomfortable in a house full of strangers, but I was also so desperately lonely that all I could do was sit in my tiny bedroom and cry. On the Monday, Mrs Farrell had to go into Northampton and offered me a lift. I went, and decided to go back home for the day, which was only a bus ride away. I couldn't bear the loneliness, and I felt so badly that I wanted to pour it all out to Mum; but I knew that I would not do so. I would make up some plausible tale about having been sent to work on the local paper, and I hoped she would not question that.

When I arrived Mum looked at me, white as a ghost, perhaps seeing me better for a weekend away from her, and fed me steak to give me some iron. I felt as if I would die if I had to go back to Mrs Farrell's, but I knew that I could not come this far without carrying through the original plan. I still felt the same way about the pain it would inflict on Mum if I were to tell her, and this way she need never know.

I returned to the wilderness of the house and settled down to await the impending arrival. On the Thursday I went to my hospital appointment, and was told off for not registering sooner; I explained the problem over changing counties, and they agreed to admit me. It was a good thing that I did not leave it any longer, because that night it happened.

I had taken too hot a bath, as always, absent-mindedly forgetting to turn off the taps, and had sunk in, grateful at being able to soothe the nagging back pain. Climbing out of the bath half an hour later I felt something trickle out of me, and looked down in time to catch the sudden flow of colourless fluid. I knew that this was the breaking of the waters, and after mopping myself up made my way to the bedroom where I packed a bag full of nightclothes and books. I was prepared for this and determined not to panic.

As I had feared, the ride to the hospital was long and uncomfortable, but eventually we arrived. As I entered the hospital, leaving Mrs Farrell to park the car, the nurse on duty looked disbelievingly at my stomach when I told her that I was in labour, and led me to a room where I was instructed to lie down and wait for the doctor. I did so, timing the contractions and blocking out all train of thought other than the purely practical one of pain and how best to relieve it. I had told the doctor at that morning's interview that I wanted an epidural for the pain, but at that moment it was not too bad.

It had been nine o'clock when the waters had broken and by eleven the contractions seemed to be getting very painful. I never cried out when I was in pain, but wondered aloud if I could have that epidural now? I was told that it was too early to give one yet, but soon, to add to the pain, there was a gaggle of students around my bed observing 'Woman in Labour'. They made the sort of noises one makes at the Tate, and I wanted to tell them that I charged for observers, but the pain intervened and I could think of nothing else. Seeing my pain, a red-haired student came over to the bed and held my hand throughout each contraction. This I was grateful for in a rather selfish way, for by squeezing his hand very very tightly I could concentrate on that and go above the pain. The look on his face each time I did so roughly equalled mine.

After what seemed truly like an eternity the nurse called the anaesthetist who gave me the much-needed epidural – painful in itself, and not helped by the fact that they told me there was always a possibility of paralysis with epidurals (they told me this *after* they had given me it). Then I sank into a semi-doze due to the drug, feeling the contractions still but only as waves of distant pain, not as searing as before. It seemed that everyone had assumed that we were in for a long night of it, because the room had emptied. I felt a sudden and insistent need to wee, and looked around the room. I rolled myself off the bed and walked drowsily to the door, pulling the foetal monitor loose without noticing. There was no one around to ask about the whereabouts of toilets, and my eye spied a little metal bowl underneath the bed. Of course! I used it. When I had finished the nurses came back in, horrified to see me out of bed. I explained my quest, and pointed to the little bowl. Silence. 'That's for swabs of cotton wool,' said the nurse.

I dozed off then, and woke some hours later to find myself well and truly on the way towards giving birth. It seemed that the baby had crept up on me while I slept, and now I was being urged to push. Push what? Everyone seemed to think that I must know all about this kind of thing. I pushed something, and a baby shot out. The midwife was amazed at the smoothness of the final stage, but told me that I had been ripped and would now have to be stitched up. First came the horrible process of the removal of the afterbirth, a slippery, dripping mass. It was put on the scales, and I wondered if they were going to try to sell it as tripe.

I lay there, still dopey from the anaesthetic, and was washed and combed into some semblance of respectability by a nurse to await the surgeon and his needle. My feet were put up in stirrups, and I was left with the door open. The surgeon certainly took his time to arrive, and every few minutes someone popped their head round the door looking for someone else, then backed out when they looked and found it was me. Eventually I was stitched, without painkillers, the doctor assuming that the epidural would still be working (it wasn't), and then I was wheeled up to the ward. The child – a boy as I had known it would be – had been cleaned and taken to the nursery, at my request. Only if I did not see him could I pretend he did not exist.

I had been promised a single room, so as not to have to look at all the proud mums with their babies, but they had no space anywhere and I ended up on the ward with everyone else. Babies were crying and fond mums were attending to them as they should be. The nursery was just yards down the corridor, and I felt that if I had to stay here long I would go mad. Every woman in the ward had an attentive husband, lover or parents around their bed, but I was alone. I drew the curtains around my bed and sat there trying to read; it was impossible.

There came a time on my second day when all the women had their babies in the ward with them, and all were asleep at siesta-time. The sound of a baby crying reached me, and I knew without doubt that it was Alex. I had called him that when in the throes of labour I went to the nursery, knowing it to be a grave mistake but unable to stay in bed when he cried, alone and the only one without a mother.

He was very small, and truly perfectly formed, old enough to be wrinkled and beetroot-coloured no longer. I picked him up, feeling instantly what I neither expected nor wanted to feel – a bonding, and a sad love. How had I been so stupid, so cruel and so blind as to have the temerity to conceive and then discard? I knew even as I stood there, *dying*, with him in my arms, that I could not keep him . . . I did not have the right to juggle him about and try to support him.

The next day, the social worker whom I disliked called at the hospital. I deliberately turned her away from the subject of Alex himself, and on to the practical matter of signing the adoption papers. I then asked the ward sister if I could leave the hospital, knowing what a terrible temptation it was to have Alex there in the same space as myself. Though warned against doing so I left the hospital that day, with a huge packet of iron tablets and strict instructions not to do too much while the stitches were still in. I had to see a midwife every day for a fortnight, as the law dictates, which meant another nine days in the wilderness, away from home.

I looked like a ghost, with a deadly pale face and brown circles under the eyes; the hospital had said this was all due to my anaemia, and warned me that my blood count was dangerously low. The biggest problem of all, however, was how to walk – the stitches were exceedingly, numbingly painful and each sudden movement brought an hour of blood and pain. I didn't help myself by trying to do sit-ups on the third day, when the leaflet had advocated their being tried on the thirtieth instead. I began to think that I would never stop bleeding – they had told me that it might last for seven weeks. How was I going to explain *that* to Mum? The midwife visited me every day at the social worker's home, and pronounced me severely anaemic, upping my dose of iron to the degree that I rattled around. I felt weak, unable to do anything without feeling very faint and dizzy. I was scared that on my return home Mum would spot something.

Come the day of my departure from the social worker's house, I lugged my heavy case to the bus station afraid of haemorrhaging – both the doctor and the midwife had warned me that this was a very real possibility, given my history of anaemia and the lack of care I was taking of myself. Mum met me at the bus stop in Brackley, took one look at me, white and wild-eyed, and ordered a taxi for the rest of the journey home. We sat in silence, she worried, looking sideways at me. My preoccupation was to get home as quickly as possible before my blood-soaked body revealed itself. She observed absent-mindedly that I was having very heavy periods again, and must go to the doctor. I nodded, and smiled wanly. The GP whom I had seen in the first place was also Mum's doctor; he had wanted to tell her of my pregnancy because he feared the strain would be too great for me to cope with alone, but I had reminded him that legally he had no right to do so as I was over sixteen years of age.

Once home I unpacked, careful to hide the iron tablets and the huge, thick sanitary towels I had to use. I reassured Mum that my pallor and lack of energy were no more than the London air sapping my health. She seemed preoccupied with something, and still depressed, although she said that she had not been lonely, and several times had seen a new friend that she had made through the church. I thought of how I had felt I was dying of loneliness and had desperately wanted to come back, and would never be able to tell her how much I had missed her, and how much I loved her . . . . These things were implicitly forbidden as topics of conversation between us. Nor could I ever break down the barrier unilaterally, for fear of an outburst of resentment against me and my long catalogue of crimes

– my inadequacies had, in the past, led her to rail against me and at the moment I was not strong enough to cope with that. As long as I kept all thoughts of Alex and what-might-have-been out of my mind I could keep my head above the waters of my own problems.

Chapter Five

In the weeks that followed the birth I alternated between the utter blackness of despair combined with a primitive longing for my child, and the realization that whatever sorrows I had now added to my list I had to get a life together and a career. My financial desires were aimed at no more than enabling me to live a simple life and to gain my freedom.

I felt that Mum had grown tired of the effort one makes to live each day when one does not see the point in life; she had no aims, no desires, and was restless, bored, lethargic. I sent off for details of Open University courses in the area to tempt her to exercise her still sharp brain, and suggested once again that she might do some voluntary work to fill her time. She received all these suggestions with a withering glance and asked me icily if I would refrain from trying to manipulate her life. She was, she added, quite capable of doing something if she wanted to. Lately I had doubted the truth of this, but was powerless to intrude where I was so obviously not wanted.

The thing I could not fathom was how she felt about and towards me; she was eternally ambivalent about everything, as was I, which made reading her thoughts rather difficult. Money was a taboo subject between us – I felt that with the £35-a-week's rent I was paying her we could afford to be less stringent about how much we spent, calculated to the last penny, on the weekly groceries, and even offered to buy my own food. But she was adamant that we should still scrimp and save – it was a long time before I discovered that having been poor once was enough to deter her from ever going down that street again. Puzzled and failing to understand, I contrasted this attitude with her strange extravagance spending money on expensive and for the most part unwearable clothes.

As time went on I became more and more aware of how tenuous were the links between us now. I saw everything with what I later realized to be distorted vision. After the birth I had felt by turns bitter, deeply saddened and confused, lost in the wilderness of my misery. I was physically unwell, having lost so much blood during the birth; because I was so anaemic my body had not replaced the precious liquid, and I felt dizzy all the time. Bending down to pick something up from the floor caused me and my stitched area immense pain, and I uttered many stifled cries during those weeks after the baby was born.

I had taken on a different job after returning from the hospital, and was now working in a supermarket loading goods in the warehouse and then lifting them on to shelves. This nearly did for me, as the weight of the goods I was lifting and the constant bending forced me to the point of exhaustion. I worked there from 1p.m. to 6p.m. every day, and at night in a restaurant from 6p.m. to midnight or whenever the customers went. I grew paler by the day and lost my appetite. After a few weeks I left the restaurant because the owners paid wages below the stated limit. I then found a night job in a pub, a real old man's pub where the customers were all regulars and drank what they insisted on being perfectly pulled pints from their own pewter tankards. One woman, a huge fat creature, drank double brandies every night from a fittingly enormous glass the size of a flower jug. The pay was little better here, but at least I had an hour's grace between my day job and this one.

I had now given up any ideas of passing my exams and concentrated on the writing I was doing for the local papers instead. My mind was so busy trying not to think of certain things such as Alex, and the fact that he simply wasn't mine any more – nor had he ever really been – that

I had no room left for studying. I was lost most of the time in a world of my own making, not able to stay in the painful cruelty of reality for too long before thoughts and memories – a child held for only a few seconds and never glimpsed again – invaded my inner sanctum of dream-like vaguenesses. I walked across roads without seeing traffic close to me, passed semi-friends by and did not see them. The general consensus was that I had either gone mad, or was getting too snooty to stay in the town. They of course did not know the truth. I had never told them at the time, and now that the disaster was past I did not see why they need know. However, troubles were close at hand.

One day in the supermarket, as I was lifting some big boxes of soap powder, I felt something turn to liquid inside me. Looking down, I saw blood beginning to seep down my legs. I passed out, luckily for me in the warehouse's darkest corner. No one saw me, and on coming to I cleaned myself up as best I could. Walking home was difficult, for the blood was now a turbulent flood that would not be contained.

Mum took one look at me and sent for the poor doctor. Terrified, I thought he would tell her of my real medical condition. He told me on no account to get out of bed, and gave me some tablets to dry up my womb; otherwise I would have to go into hospital for a small operation to clean it out. I agreed, fingers crossed behind my back, to stay in bed, and as soon as he had gone I got up. It seemed that Mum did not know. She came towards me, flapping with anxiety. 'Please go back to bed! You're not thinking of going to work tonight, surely?'

I replied that there was no question of me missing an evening – I might lose my job. Before going, I asked her if the doctor had mentioned anything to her.

She looked at me, puzzled. 'No. Why? What's the matter with you? What is it? Why did you bleed so much?'

There and then I made the decision that I had to tell her before she wore herself out with worrying, but I approached the subject in a cowardly way. 'You know when I went on that course, and you wondered what I had spent all that money on?'

She nodded, wary.

'I went away to have a baby. It was the result of a rape ....'

At the last minute, I had resorted to that old story instead of the truth. She could only take a certain amount in one go, after all. To tell her not only that I had had a baby, but also that I had defied all the laws of the Church, would be too cruel, and I did not have the courage to say that.

She stood immobile, in a shocked stance. Then she turned to me, and I was afraid for the first time that she might lose control and lash out at me. She looked at me with bewilderment. She tried to speak but could not, for a while, and for the first time in years, the first time, we hugged, for mutual comfort, our bodies fitting strangely against each other, the contact odd and uneasy, a form of truce.

Then she broke away, mouth trembling. 'How could you have had a baby? When? I ... I don't see when, or how ....'

I hated to go on, and wished desperately that I had not told her, but reflected rapidly that it might be better coming from my mouth than from the doctor's, a stranger and an outsider. It was a long silence. I heard the rain tripping desultorily against the double-glazed windows, and thought how to tell her the rape story. I did so quietly, without drama, with guilt, with self-hatred, but almost with justification, feeling that all my previous sexual experience had been rape with consent, for which there can be no charge.

She nodded as she listened, remarking that I had always been one for going off alone without thought for the consequences. She remained standing while I recited the barrage of lies – and then, to my amazement, she began to cry. Not loudly, just a hurt, soft, broken sobbing. She could not believe that all the turbulent events of the past few months had taken place without her knowing, or guessing something.

I started to explain how I had thought it best to hide this from her because she seemed so fragile, so worn, so world-weary, and I had not the heart to add to her burden of disappointments with my last-straw tale.

She turned to me, face awry with lack of understanding, and asked me, quietly, if I had not been able to tell her because in truth she was, and had been, a bad mother. I was shocked that she should think like this. Sinking into a chair, she said that she had not been supportive to me when I had had the 'bad times' with the suicide attempts and the depression, and she had not been there for my guidance when Dad had died.

I was surprised that she had invoked his name. She seemed to shrink, sitting there so forlornly, a lost soul indeed. I touched her, awkwardly, feeling uneasy in this new-found role of accuser rather than accused. There seemed to be no way to convince her that my motive had been purely to save her from the shame and pain of unnecessary knowledge. I told her, in vain, that even if she had known, there was nothing, absolutely nothing, she could have done.

She looked up at me, eyes cold, face crumpling into lines of sorrow, betrayal, mistrust. 'I am no use,' she said, with finality in her voice. 'No use at all, not even as a mother, which is all I know how to be now.'

What could I say? I left her to ruminate, neither of us sure of our ground, her thoughts confused, unable to blame, but feeling resentment at my unintentional proof of her failure. I thought to myself that if this was true, and she had failed in her maternal duties, we were a good pair, for at everything else in life I had failed. There was not much further down the ladder of spiralling disaster and wrong-doing I could go. Or so I thought.

From the day of revelations onwards, we lived in almost completely separate worlds. I went to my jobs, and tried in hopeless misery and deepest frustration to marshal my thoughts towards revision for the looming exams; I cared nothing for the results, but was desperate to achieve some little success to appease Mum's prophecy that I would never do any good. It was hopeless; I could not tear my thoughts away from the revulsion of self that

I felt for having told Mum, and thus condemned her to a life of misery and self-derision.

Often in those days I would come home from work to find her sitting in the chair by the window in the semi-dark, gazing out at nothing. When I asked what was she looking at, in an attempt to make conversation lightly, pleasantly, she turned to face me and I saw stale tears chasing down her parchment cheeks. 'I'm looking at my past,' she said, and I saw, perhaps for the first time, how the weeks of knowledge had taken their toll. 'I'm looking at the wreck my life is, and the sham we hide behind, you and me.' It was true. We spent some of the little free time I had together, going to the little town to shop, to drink coffee, to make conversation we didn't have, to be the apparently happy mother and daughter we were no longer. I felt bleak, a stranger, uncertain of my future, unsure of my sanity.

More and more I thought about Alex, despite my anguished attempts to force him out of my mind. I had to go to the social worker to settle the details of the adoption – she produced a list of 'suitable people', and without delay discarded those on the list who were obviously working-class – the lorry driver, the milkman, the butcher. I was aghast – she did not regard me as working-class, even though that was what I was, but as middle-class, and was pretentious enough to decide that Alex should go, in this lottery-like, baby-farming arrangement, to a similar home. I felt sickened, and tried desperately to think of some other way, but I still could not see how I could support him properly without a steady job and a home of my own. I knew nothing about alternatives to adoption, naïve as that may sound, and was ignorant of arrangements such as short-term foster care, which might have given me more time to consider how to keep Alex and support him. So I had to continue to discuss the new 'parents' with artificial enthusiasm while the almost criminally tactless social worker spoke patronizingly in a whispery grandmother tone of Alex as 'Baby' ('Well, I've seen Baby today, and he looks very well. Would you like a photo of him?') and me as 'Mummy'. I gritted my teeth and waited until the interview was over, then rushed outside for fresh air after the staleness of the social services office.

I never cried after Alex was born, afraid that if I once started to let the pain out it would flood my soul and leave me too battered and bruised emotionally to cope with the jungle of everyday life. In fact, on reflection I never allowed myself any form of release from my well of pain, or mourning for my lost son. I played no sports, which might have released my aggression; I wrote very factual copy, so I had no creative outlets there; I had no close friends in whom I would confide, or family to whom I might have gone. I would not dream of breaking down in front of Mum, because she had her own bundle of problems to cope with, and would not have known what to do if I had let the mask slip for a moment. Tears were near the surface most of the time, but that was where they stayed.

At the pub where I worked, the landlord cruelly bet one of the regulars that he could get me to go out with him. (They were curious as to why I never accepted any of the inevitable offers, many unsavoury, that any barmaid receives.) I refused tearfully and made my way home, holding in the lump of choking pain, until I came to a dark alley near my house. I cried all the way home from there onwards, until I neared the house when I dried my eyes and presented my cheery false exterior to Mum.

In the chair, in the dark, I faced once again a torrent of wrathful, unreasoning abuse from her. She had taken to this form of self-release of late, storing up her grievances until, bursting with old resentment and anger, she poured them upon me as I came in the door. I had even learned to switch off, because I knew almost exactly what she would say next. The frustrated hatreds and disappointments that had built up over the years were being well aired now – my inability to be anything a daughter should be, my school disasters, my record of attendance, my failed exams, and now this last, final, cruel piece of punishment to be heaped upon her by a selfish, stupid, cold-hearted ingrate was too much to be borne silently.

I watched her as she spoke, not looking at me, but

at the many ghosts of regret from her past, the long-silenced bitterness at her brothers and sisters, who she felt had abandoned her for the most part; bitterness at the failure of a daughter who had had such great expectations heaped upon her head and had not delivered the goods; at her husband, long dead, whose inability to give her what she thought she wanted still rankled. She spoke like this, harshly, cruelly, in a monotone, for some time. I knew that she had stopped caring about life after I had told her my story, and she even mentioned on these sort of occasions that she had no further wish to live, since life held nothing for her except the onset of old age, the remaining enemy to strip her of her faculties and her dignity. To these death-wish pronouncements she made an addendum that of course, because of her still-strong faith in God, she could never commit such a sin. I understood Mum's reasons for speaking as she did to me, and where her bitterness came from, but that made the nightly tirades no easier to cope with. We had agreed after my 'confession' that we would not discuss Alex and would act as if it had not happened, our usual way of dealing with a major crisis. It was a mutual disinclination to face a problem we did not like the look of – unhealthy, but a staunch family tradition.

She seemed to grow smaller, less defined, as she went about her daily business, to the locals a curious creature, locked up and refusing to acknowledge my presence if she felt particularly vindictive. I wondered if her ever-present thyroid condition might be playing up. She took several pills every morning which I guessed were for that, to regulate her hormone levels. She was depressed, apathetic, lethargic, bored and yet reluctant to try to change her life, to move house perhaps, to get a job, to do some voluntary work, to join clubs and meet people with similar tastes to her own . . . she felt too old and used, she said wearily, to be bothered with anything like that.

I was at a loss about what to suggest to salvage her from the wreck of her own life – she was sixty-one, still young enough to make new areas of life for herself. It was no good, I realized, trying to do things for her if her heart was not in it. I had made all the obvious suggestions many times over. As a well-meaning kid, I even applied for jobs I thought she would like and then waited, breathless with excitement, for the letter to drop through the door. When it did, offering Mum an interview for a position she knew nothing about, she was furious rather than pleasantly surprised.

I learned to draw upon myself, become emotionally self-sufficient. I spoke to no one, least of all Mum, because I was scared of starting off one of the storms inadvertently. I decided that my way to get over the loss of Alex was to be self-punishment; I would do whatever I found unpleasant, painful even. I had several minor haemorrhages during my heavy job at the supermarket, but carried on regardless. Besides, the more I worked, the less time I had to think about my personal trials and tribulations. I worked most nights at the pub, hardly speaking to the customers in case I released my verbal aggression on one of them. I felt as if some strength of purpose was forcing me to a breakdown, or to disappear in a puff of smoke, so great and far-reaching was my pain and anger and frustration.

Friday, 27 June 1986 was a fairly ordinary day. I went to work in the same daze with which I did most things at that time, stifled grief and unexplained rage producing a muffled dopiness, another world for me to live in while the real world, loud and cruel, revolved around me. As I crossed the road on the way home I nearly got run over; forgetting to look for traffic was a common trait of mine then. Arriving at home I took a deep breath and walked in, awaiting the customary verbal onslaught. Mum seemed to be at a pitch of fury, cold and blazing, that night; sitting there thinking all day, ruminating upon what might have been, what could have been, what should have been, she had had plenty of time to work herself up into a frenzy. I was told how cold, how heartless I was, leaving her alone all day and all night, and for what? To work like some slut in a pub and a supermarket, demeaning myself and her. She would not shop in the supermarket, in case anyone realized that she had a daughter who worked there. The usual refrain followed – the litany about the family, how it had grown so far apart, how I had disgraced her in every way, making it appear that she was a bad mother when the blame lay only with me, when she had given up so much to let me always have the best, and still I turned round and disgraced her. I had not achieved any of her planned successes. I had always been too headstrong and selfish, wanting to be independent – well, she would see how independent I could be when she cut me off without a penny, and so on, and so on, and so on.... I listened, dully, trying to tune out the worst of what she was saying, having heard it all before. I never, never answered back – it would only have inflamed her even more.

I wanted to go to bed, but was trembling with something like rage and fear. I slept very little these days, for my head was too full of other things, too worried, too depressed, too other-worldly. We had developed a peculiar routine, even though we were so far apart – Mum slept badly too, so if we were both awake an uneasy truce would be formed and, at her request, I would move a camp-bed into her room and lie there talking about safe, unemotional matters until we eventually drifted into some semblance of sleep. I suppose that even if I irritated and saddened her in daylight, in the darkness she could not see my face and I could be anybody, impersonal, to whom she was talking.

That night we went to bed, both hot and cold with anger and all sorts of unknown things lurking beneath the surface. I went into my room and lay in bed, fruitlessly trying to relax enough to sleep a little. Eventually she called out for me to come in and sleep on the camp-bed. I obeyed, hoping for no more accusations. We talked desultorily, not feeling sleepy. I got up and went for a wander around the house, the nearest thing to pacing up and down that can be done in a small bungalow. I went into my bedroom to look out of the window... everything was very grey. I had had times like this before, when everything seemed to be colourless, odourless, static, grey. I felt as though I could not move properly.

And in the bedroom on my dressing table lay a hammer. It was there as part of a still life collection of objects I had been drawing – some hats, a knife, a pear, a brick. Here I will say only what I can bear to, what I feel is possible for me to tell. I have thought and thought and I can see nothing good to be gleaned from the details of the act that happened. I killed my mother. The past cannot be whitewashed by reconstruction, and it is never far from my mind anyway, whatever I am doing, wherever I am, whoever I am with. It always haunts me and I pay for it every day, with all my heart's pain and memory that is too vivid for peace or comfort . . . .

It was I, suddenly galvanized into action, who picked up the phone and called the police, my voice sounding strange and alien to me. I stood for a few minutes and saw nothing, heard nothing but whirls of horror. I told the police there had been a burglar. I moved, ghostlike, into the room and started to pull things out of drawers haphazardly. Scarves, the jewellery box, clothes. I was sick in the bathroom. A dog barked. I went outside into the moonlight and walked in circles on the lawn. Everything still grey. Too grey to see properly. I thought absurdly of a song that Dad used to sing to me when I was a kid: 'Round and Round the Mulberry Bush'. At some point I went round to the back door and collided with a neighbour to whom I whimpered: 'Something – I've done something terrible – terrible's happened – look at the blood.' (He told the police that this was what I had said. I can't remember.) Then he went inside his house to phone the police.

Then, I phoned my uncle Ken, automatically, and told him, he says, that I had killed her. He must be right. Again, I have no recollection of this. He told me to stay there and said he was on his way. Everyone seemed to arrive at once. Many policemen, a WPC, my uncle and aunt, and the neighbour and his dog. I was taken to the sitting room and told by one of the policemen to sit down, not to touch anything and not to move. I watched them as they watched me with one eye, chatting desultorily among themselves while they waited for their inspector to come to the scene. They laughed softly, joked amongst themselves, gossiped about others at work and relationships. I caught flickers of words that meant nothing to me. My aunt put a coat over my knees to cover up my bare legs in case the men should look at me. The detectives asked to use the phone. One was kind. I heard a policeman say on the phone, 'Get the cell ready. It's a naughty one.' They asked me softly, warily, what had happened.

'We were going into Oxford tomorrow,' I said. 'Can we still go?'

They looked at each other. I was led into the kitchen and sat down with a dour, beareded PC to look after me. I sat, nauseous, while detectives and other men swarmed around me. I looked at the blood on my legs and felt the sickness swim right to the front of my mind, the edges blurry now. My mouth was dry. My knees trembled. Cold. Feet bare on the kitchen lino. Laughter still occasionally drifted in from the rest of the house, ghostlike, disembodied.

After a while the WPC came to relieve the man. She asked me questions softly too, persistently, firmly. What had I been doing that evening? Had I been feeling depressed or in a bad mood? Had we argued? Had I seen anyone come into the house? Had anything gone missing? I told her, I think, that it had been a man, that I had not seen him properly, that he must have . . . and then I could not say anything more, and the questions stopped. As we sat there I denied consistently and steadily any knowledge of what had happened. It was my sanity at stake now as I blanked out what I had done and my part in it.

After that I was led away, unprotesting, to the front hall, via my bedroom where one of the detectives told me to put some clothes on. Then I was led through the silent street and ushered into an unmarked car.

It was 2a.m. when we arrived at Northampton police station, where I was led to the rape suite. To be examined, I was told. Standard procedure. I was told to strip and to wait for the police surgeon. I stood naked, under the penetrating gaze of the WPC, with detectives passing by the open door. This did not seem odd to me, and I stood like a frozen work of art, incapable and undesiring of movement. It was 4a.m. before the doctor came to examine me and take swabs. He noticed the thick menstrual blood trickling suddenly down my thighs, red and dark and strong. I had forgotten that I was due that day.

He looked at me with kind eyes, strangely compassionate. I was confused. Pity? He asked me if I ever had pre-menstrual tension. I did not really know exactly what he meant. He could tell that I had recently had a child, and asked me about that. I told him. He smiled tiredly, and told me, patting my shoulder, that he would give me something to help me sleep when the time for sleep eventually came, and that he would see me afterwards. After what? I was allowed to have a shower and to put on the clothes I had dazedly picked up on my way out of the house.

It was a hot night, but I shivered in the chilliness of the underground building. I was taken to the interview room where the two detectives sat. They greeted me, standing, and I thought how formal it was. They told me in mechanical voices that now I would have a chance to tell them what had happened. Someone mentioned a solicitor. I knew nothing about them, or my rights. One was found, and asked to attend. He was called Roy, and was well respected and admired by the police, who told me that I couldn't have a better brief. What was a brief? One of the men brought me a blanket to ease my shivers. I was bleeding heavily. Roy told me what he thought about the situation I was in, and asked me what had really happened. I told him, voice wobbling dangerously, what I had told the WPC at the house. He removed his glasses and rubbed his eyes wearily.

'Anna – I am now your legal representative and I have to work on your behalf. If you are not telling me the truth how can I represent you fairly?

I shook my head. He didn't understand. How could he? If I told the truth, I would have to acknowledge to myself what I had done, and I could not do that. My stomach began to turn over once more. I was given coffee, strong and sweet, and offered cigarettes. I thought of the corny old films where the detectives always have a bad guy and a good guy, and then I began to feel afraid and for the first time, with a huge and overwhelming sense of pain, I became aware of how alone I was.

The detectives were honest and kind, and I didn't know what to say. They wrote down every word I did say, my untruthful and faltering account, and Roy sat with his head in his hands. I went on calm, stony-faced and controlled as long as I kept the hideous reality from me.

After two hours of this the detectives looked at me, and I looked at Roy, and realized that I could not go on with this. I asked for a moment alone with him, and they agreed willingly. When they had gone I broke down and told Roy the truth. I spared him nothing. He stopped me whilst I was in full flow and asked me to tell the detectives all that I had told him.

Back in the interview room, the detectives were more than happy to make a fresh statement. 'Where do you want to begin?'

'At the beginning. It starts a long time ago, though . . . . '
'That's OK. Take your time. We're in no hurry.'

I gave them the whole story, and it took hours. I told them of the killing, the aftermath, the panic, the disbelief that it had been me, the thoughts I had had. We seemed to have been there, in that small, smoky room, for ever. I had cried myself sick, drunk too much coffee, was still bleeding and still cold.

'You have the right to eight hours' rest in every twenty-four hours of detainment,' one of them told me. 'Do you wish to take the rest or continue?'

I continued until I had nothing left to tell them and had answered all of their questions and a few of my own. Then I needed to rest.

'I want to lie down now, please – the doctor said he would give me something.'

I was taken to a cell, cold and dark and dirty, heavy with the stench of stale urine and cold vomit. I sank on to the metal bed, clutching the iron-grey blankets around me. But before I could sleep, the detectives came into the cell and formally charged me.

'Anna Louisa Reynolds, you are charged with the following offence: murder. That on the twenty-seventh day of June in the year of 1986 you did murder one Elizabeth Catherine Reynolds, aged sixty-one, both of 38 Roman Way, Brackley. You are charged on this indictment and will be taken to a court of law to answer the charge, where you will be given the opportunity to ask for bail.'

Then they left me, the doctor gave me some potent pills, and I slept the sleep of the drugged.

In due course I was woken by the policewoman and told that I had a visitor. The previous evening I had made several phone calls and told people where I was being held. My visitor now was Alan's mum, Pat, whom I had rung because Alan was due back on leave that day and I wanted him to know that I was not at home. She had rushed over from Coventry to the police station, and was lost for words. When she was told by the desk sergeant what I had been charged with, she had not believed him. Now she did. She asked me if it was true, and I nodded mutely. We talked of things, trivial things, but I was still dopey from the drug and was not very lucid. She realized at once that I was in shock and was careful not to bring me out of it. She tells me that I told her Mum and I were supposed to be in Oxford and asked why they were keeping me there.

Next I saw my aunt and uncle, the ones who had come to the house, with my other aunt and cousin. I was not able to say a lot, but my aunts cried and asked why. I told them about the baby, and they asked why I had not been able to go and tell them about it. I did not answer. The aunt whom I had not seen for a long time was later to describe me as 'very cool and calm, very self-assured' during that visit.

When they had gone I lay down and tried to think of anything but the killing. I talked to the matron whom the police had sent to keep an eye on me – a large, maternal lady who was at first suspicious of me because I was, she said, too quiet, then took to me, was fiercely protective, let me use the phone to call the family and made me many cups of strong, sweet tea.

Roy came to see me, and told me that I would be appearing next morning in front of the local magistrates, to be remanded in custody until reports assessing my mental state could be made.

'What do they mean – isn't this custody? Can't I stay here?' (No one had actually said the word 'prison' yet.)

'No, Anna,' he said in a kindly way, as one would talk to an idiot child, 'I'm afraid that custody means prison, Holloway Prison, in London. You'll be all right there, I promise, I've made arrangements for you to be put on the hospital wing, the psychiatric part, where you'll be looked after by doctors and nurses, and be given all the help I think you need.'

I was not reassured. In the Sunday paper the matron had just given me there was an article about a local woman who had just done three months inside Holloway Prison, and the tales she told were horrific. Scrubbing floors all day long with the officer's foot on your back, lesbians all of them. Drugs forced upon young girls just like me. Violence perpetrated as a daily occurrence.

The next morning I was taken to court with four other girls in a dank, smelly van driven badly by a young policeman who chatted kindly to me. He told me not to worry and asked the other girls what Holloway was like. They all laughed and joked raucously, and turned to me, curiously, asking me what was I in for. I looked at them blankly and said I didn't understand. 'What have you done? What crime you done to be going to the nick?'

I swallowed, and thought about it. I couldn't even say the word 'murder', let alone explain who and how. I was about to make up a ridiculous lie when we arrived at the court room and were told to get out of the van. I was led into another cold, dirty cell and told that I would be 'up' at 10a.m.

At the appointed time I was taken into the court room and led to the dock. I looked around and saw the detectives, my uncle, my aunts and cousin, and some reporters on the press bench. Roy spoke briefly about how he was not applying for bail at this time, because he felt I needed to be assessed by the prison medical staff before we decided where I would go if given bail at a later date. The magistrates peered at me and asked me if I would like to sit down since I looked very pale. Roy then outlined the case to them and told them of the offence, at which point everyone in the court winced and I tore up a handkerchief in agony.

At last the ordeal was over and I was taken back to the cell until the van came to transport me to Holloway. I sat and thought of the tales I had read in the newspaper about the prison, and of the rough, sharp girls in the van on the way to court. I crouched on the floor in the corner of the cell, waiting for the next stage of my journey.

Chapter Six

It was a hot June day – too hot for the police, who sweated profusely in their thick uniforms. I blinked as we emerged into the sun from the underground depths of the cells, eyes closed against the unwelcome brightness. We went not in a van, but in a marked car, accompanied by one of the detectives who had interviewed me, and a policewoman. As we drove into the fringes of London, we stopped at a garage where the driver bought us all an ice cream. Mine melted as I held it, dripping on to my fingers which were sticky in the humidity.

'Eat up,' said the jolly, red-faced WPC. 'It'll be the last one of those that you'll see for a long time. Make the most of it. They won't give you treats inside like we do – they're not soft.'

With these heartening words we neared our destination. I saw signs pointing to Holloway, then to the prison itself. I could see nothing that resembled the only visions I had, which were of the grey stone towers of the Scrubs in *Porridge*. The area was scruffy, with piles of rubbish on the streets.

'There,' said the policewoman, pointing. 'There's your home for the next few weeks, love. Don't look so sad! It's not so bad, is it? Looks a bit like a sports centre to me.'

To me, Holloway looked only like the prison that it was, a large, spreading, modern building of red brick, with tall windows and even taller gates at the perimeter. We drove in and waited in the middle of a forecourt for another two gates to open – it was obvious that, for this to happen, there was some sort of password which the hapless policeman did not know, to his embarrassment. I watched in distracted fascination as his neck turned purply-red. I felt sorry for him. He was only young.

We waited until an exasperated-looking officer in blue garb with epaulettes proclaiming 'HMP' came towards us. The second courtyard looked less foreboding – a bright green door marked 'Receptions' led to a corridor of duller green. To my left, in the yard, I could see two big wooden gates opening slowly, reluctantly, a pair of giant, creakily arthritic twins. Three women emerged from the giants dressed in ordinary clothes, wearing bands of blue material on their arms.

I was pushed gently towards the Receptions door. I thought of a hotel I had once been to – the only hotel I had ever been to – where I had gone to a reception and was welcomed with glasses of sherry and little trays of nuts and crisps. That thought was rudely pushed aside as my pitiful bag of belongings was thrown on to the floor and left there. My reaction, to move towards it, was sharply curbed by the grim-faced officer who was taking down my 'details' from the police. I stood ashen, seeing myself for the first time in a mirror of perspex.

'Name?'

'Anna.'

'I meant surname.'

'Oh . . . Reynolds, Anna Reyno— '

'Right. You're D, got that? D28286. Don't forget that.'

I was told to take a dressing gown from the pile and go and strip, then put on the wretched moth-eaten article. Where was I to change? I was led to a tiny, filthy cubicle by a tall, thin officer whose voice was extraordinarily loud – or so I thought until we rounded the corner and I was assailed by the combined noise of what appeared to be hundreds of girls and women, some uniformed, some half-naked, some seeming not to be in full control of their faculties. The air reeked of vomit, of stale and fresh urine, of smoke and, strangely, disinfectant, school corridor-style.

I was led through this jungle of humanity to the cubicle

where I changed, slowly, numbly, while the ever-watchful officer stood outside. I opened the door and was told sharply to stay inside and sit down until I was called for.

Timidly I asked how long for.

She couldn't say, there were forty-six women to 'process' before me. It had been a busy day. Mondays were always busy, she reflected, crossing her long, thin legs at the ankles as she stood leaning against the wall; it was all the ones who were nicked on Friday nights and stayed in police cells over the weekends.

She left me to my waiting, and I sat gingerly on the butt-strewn bench of ash-marked wood, in the stringy scrap of brown material, clothes clutched close to me, feet bare and toes curling on the filthy floor, flesh goose-pimpled with cold and anticipation. I was tired... my eyes felt hollow.

The door opened and I shrank back with fear. A short, stocky woman stood there, a bored, resigned expression on her face.

'You Reynolds?'

'Yes... yes.'

'You want some tea? There's no vegetarian left, only ham.' She nodded at the plate in her hand.

'Oh... what time is it, please?'

'Six o'clock. Stick them plates outside when you're finished with them.'

Cold, slimy ham, more fat than meat. Large, congealing, greasy chips, also cold. A bowl of stiff, cold rice pudding, of a texture like concrete, perched upon the edge of the tired blue plastic plate. I rejected it, repelled. Tea! A warming, gratefully received mug, also plastic, pockmarked but filled with blissfully hot, sweet tea. I had not thought they would give sugar in prison. I drank, warming my hands on the cup.

Needing the loo, I ventured outside the door of the cubicle and was spotted by the officer.

'Back inside! Where d'you think *you're* going?'

I explained hesitantly, feeling like a schoolgirl once more begging to use the toilet as an escape from a lesson.

A minute later the silent tea-bearer led me to another

cubicle, this time without a perspex window, thankfully. At least I could pee in peace.

The wait ended at seven o'clock, when I was summoned to the main room. Officers sat at desks, talking loudly and raucously. A mat stood in one corner. I was told to stand upon it ('Not for the sake of your feet but in case you pass something infectious on to one of us . . . . ') and take off my dressing gown. I did so, feeling a passing flush of shyness and mild embarrassment which fled into dullness. 'Knickers off!' barked a large, stout officer, man-like. I obeyed, feeling soulless, too tired and numb to care about such things as degradation. I was turned around. 'Give us a twirl. Don't be shy now!' There were touches of coyness at this point from the officers, who looked up and down, poked and prodded. I was then told to put my dressing gown back on and stand where I was while my meagre bundle of belongings was sorted through.

'Too many pairs of knickers – you're allowed four. Choose. And too many pairs of socks – where did you think you were coming to? Thinking of staying a while, were you?'

I was issued with the staples of the prison welfare kit: a bar of harsh green soap, a rough white flannel, an even rougher cardboard nightdress, and a toothbrush with a little brown paper bag (the kind you put used sanitary towels in – it had that advertised upon the front). On inspection the bag proved to contain a scented green powder which I immediately assumed to be soap powder for knicker-washing (even I was not naïve enough to think that there would be a laundry service in a prison). In fact it turned out to be tooth powder. I was mystified – how could one achieve clean teeth with a mouthful of powder? It would not stay on the brush.

Then I was beckoned towards a sign proclaiming 'Bat'. This meant bath-time; the missing 'h', I soon learnt, symbolized the absent hot water. Dirty, dirty bathtub! I recoiled in horror. Little black hairs decorated the plughole. Black ring around the tub. Cigarette ends strewn over the blackened floor. A tin of bath cleaner and a mangled scouring pad stood nearby. I grimaced and set to.

Later, after a two-inch immersion in lukewarm water, I emerged, slightly cleaner, with a damp head, seal-like. I was put into another cubicle, this time a locked one. I asked why, and was told by the warder it was because they had to take precautions with me. 'You'll be taken to the psychiatric unit, you see, and we don't want you to do anything silly while you're down here with us.'

I wanted to talk to her and reassure myself that she had no horns and no third eye in the middle of her forehead like some would believe. Or was that only the prisoners they thought that about?

'You're in here for a really serious crime, aren't you? If I were you I wouldn't tell any of the women on the wing what you've done.' As if I could even admit the full and loathsome horror to myself. 'Tell them you're in for a drugs offence or something. It's easier that way, otherwise they'll want to know all about it. Dead nosey they'll be.'

I looked at her.

'Don't upset yourself now. We all feel that way sometimes about people close to us. God knows I do . . . . You seem like a good kid – what happened? . . . . You don't have to tell me if you don't want to. I'm just curious 'cause you seem to have everything going for you . . . pretty, young, intelligent. What *did* happen?'

Luckily I was saved from having to reply by the ominous sight of what was obviously a chief among the many Indians looming towards us. Hastily and unceremoniously I was locked in and left alone once more. I still felt nothing except a growing weariness and a desire to lay my head to rest somewhere.

After a truly interminable wait I was taken to see the doctor, a man with pale, uninterested eyes and a weary face. He looked me up and down as if I were a museum exhibit and expressed an interest in my 'case'. Then he launched straight into a detailed resumé of the murder, watching me carefully, fiercely, for a reaction.

I was still numb: it was, after all, only the Monday after the Friday. I asked him for some help with sleeping.

He agreed, cautiously, to give me a few nights' medication. They would be wanting, he said, to test me out, to see if I slept without the aid of drugs.

Was that supposed to be the sign of a clear conscience, or of a lack of remorse? The sign of a murderer or a madwoman, a psychopath?

I would be watched, he said, for a clue as to why I did what I did. They wanted to find out what made me tick.

I, for my part, said nothing, justifiably fearful of open interpretation. But he interpreted the silence, too... nothing was sacred.

Out of the doctor's office and in to the nurse; here I was weighed, measured, and all but stamped and posted. Then I was sent back to my little cubicle – to wait, of course. I got no answers to my tentative questions about where I was going.

The psychiatric wing was not, I quickly realized, ward-like. When I was led there, slowly, as if to the noose, it was more like a spaceship. Bad fluorescent lighting and dark, murky corridors led away to even darker, murkier cells, their walls blackened in the half-light of the night by blood, shit, unidentifiable dirt and doors painted the colour of despair. Hopelessness wafted from these walls as I passed along them ghost-like. I felt the dullness in me sink to impenetrable depths as I was pushed gently into a large cell, a dormitory in which lay four other women sleeping the heavy, sterterous sleep of the drugged.

Once again I was stripped, turned around and handed back my clothes. The door was slammed to, and I stood silently on the floor in the middle of the room, clutching my clothes to me, naked and paralysed by exhaustion. The moonlight coloured the other women grey and silver, and the barred windows cast strange lines of light and darkness over the beds. Two women woke up at the sound of the heavy door. One studied me with sleep-filled eyes. She was young, with a halo of brown hair standing out from her head. The other wore sunglasses of blue plastic, and in the freakishness of the moment I wondered if the prison had supplied them to match the mugs and plates.

A nurse came to the door and peered at me through the open hatch which let a cold breeze shiver its way to us. She handed me a tiny pot of vile green liquid and watched me carefully to see that I took it all and did not try to hold it in my mouth. I drank it down thankfully and then showed her my tongue, hoping for a midnight cessation of pained memories.

I made the bed up with the sheets and bedcover I had been given and found the cold, semi-clean sheets soothing. I slid inside, curled up foetus-like for comfort, and slept.

I have only the haziest of memories of the next two or three days. I was still in that numb state where things, people, names and events register at the time but do not remain in the mind. It was delayed reaction, I suppose, but the result is that a whole piece of my memory is missing.

After possibly a week or so, I began to come back to life a little. I learned the stories of my cell companions, and they began to seem like real people to me, whereas before they had been only figures in a mist. I learned the routine and daily pattern of life on C1, as it was called. I knew nothing of its notorious history, or of the inadequate treatment the desperately sick women received.

Soon I met the doctor and the psychiatrist who were to make reports upon me; both were eventually to play large parts in my fate. The doctor was a dark, large man with a pale, unappetizing complexion. He was Himmler-like in tall black boots, dark glasses and a black leather coat. I was instantly wary of him, and the feeling was mutual. He regarded me with the same kind of curious intensity coupled with dislike which the receptions doctor had displayed.

The psychiatrist was different. He treated me as if I were a free individual, and gave no hint of any discrimination towards me or assumptions of guilt or blame. He was Irish, personable, unthreatening and *normal*. He also refused to have a nurse in the room when we talked. The usual wing practice was for a posse of them to be present 'just in case' one of us attacked the doctors. We had regular sessions, three a week at least; they were useful on his part for the report he was making for the court, whilst for me it was invaluable to be able to talk in a trustworthy environment, to cry if I had to, to release my burden on to the strong arms of a professional. If only I had had such an opportunity before... I didn't often let myself think wistful, weak thoughts like that nowadays.

Being on the wing was like walking into looking-glass land. The first impression, in daytime, was of bedlam: women roamed the landings, some half-dressed, some not dressed at all and yet others wearing perhaps some outlandish array of garments from the forties. Judges and magistrates came to view the wing quite often, and were herded through pretty fast if some woman was considered to be 'making an exhibition' of herself. The unpleasantness of life on C1 was swept hastily under the carpet of ignorance. You don't really want to see that crazy woman banging her head against the wall, do you? It was very frustrating to hear the legal hierarchy pass through the wing and hear their comments ('Oh, how nice – they have en suite bathrooms.' This from a Hertfordshire magistrate on seeing the cells with a steel toilet, stinking, filthy and not working, plus a basin coated with blood and other substances.)

I felt a curious alliance with the other women; and instead of regarding each other with suspicion we greeted each other, even as strangers, with a positive solidarity, a silent support and acknowledgement. Yet suspicion was there briefly when a stranger treated the comparative shelter of our makeshift home with contempt or created a threat.

My companions in the dormitory were beginning to develop in front of me like photographic negatives, revealing aspects of themselves and their lives as we began to trust each other enough to unlock some of our mutual and much-needed defences. I delved into their worlds, different from mine, different from each other's, as a means of losing myself in them and delaying facing myself. It worked.

Marlene, who was about forty-four, told me her story. I listened, fascinated as a voyeur. 'I'm a lesbian, I think. I mean, I've never done anything – you know, never done it – but I've been living with my Andy for years. She's twenty years older than me. The other day I tried to smother her with a pillow. She didn't die, though. She just woke up and said, "Oh darling, darling, whatever are you doing?" I was so frightened. I went to pieces and ran away. She called the police. She was scared of me, they said. They brought me here then. You know, it's funny, I even came here for a job once. They turned me down, said I was too little. Then they found out anyway that I had a criminal record.'

Her 'criminal record' was a suicide attempt from the days when it was an offence to try to take your own life. She had, it transpired, been in and out of various mental institutions since she was a child. Marlene and I worked together as kitchen girls – no matter how old women in prison are, they are always called 'girls'. I puzzled over this for a time, then realized that it is a subtle way to diminish a woman by referring to her as a child – even if the diminisher is also a woman. To judges and magistrates we were either 'girls' or 'ladies' – at least, that was how we would be addressed. Girlies need smacked bottoms, don't they, and ladies fall from grace and must be reprimanded, and then given back to the care of her husband, because, as one High Court judge said he had been told by a probation officer, 'female offenders often make good mothers, but of course no man wants them after they have offended. A shame, because with a husband and children to look after she will be too busy to commit crime. And if she is tempted, her husband may just tell her to stop it.' Which in one easy lesson shows you all you need to know about women who commit crime.

The view of a seasoned prison officer, however, is that 'they're just like children, you see, they're very childlike... you wouldn't talk to a four-year-old the way we talk to them, sometimes.' It *was* true that some of the women on C1 were childlike in their behaviour, their surprised and affronted innocence. We were all regarded by the rest of the prison as idiots; C1 was known as the Muppet House for that reason. The screams, chants, wails, continual crying, banging of heads, of windows, of hatches, of chairs, perpetrated the myth that we were all lost souls.

I was content to be so labelled, hovering between

wanting to believe that I too was possibly mad, and knowing that I was not, but the anonymity of the 'insane' label enabled me to opt out of trying to preserve a front of normality. Marlene and I passed as 'normal' on the wing – we were, perhaps, the least eccentric (although I do think that her wearing of sunglasses in the dead of night, in bed, could be called eccentric). We were certainly the quietest, politest, most sickeningly well-behaved women ever to have graced the shit-corroded walls of Holloway. Neither of us had the sense to see the traps we were setting ourselves for the future. We both had a litany of awful memories, and yet the prison created in us a false sense of security, at odds with the reality we would one day have to face again.

We distanced ourselves from the real world. Each of us had known from the beginning that we were not strong enough to face it unarmoured. Once in jail, although we sometimes forgot that was where we were in the midst of C1's chaos and confusion, we were safe and protected. We welcomed the childlike treatment that we received – no responsibilities, no material fears or financial desperation. It was not, primarily, these responsibilities which we wished to shy from, but the ability to make decisions had left us along with our freedom.

I saw the assigned prison doctor every day, and I relied on him – his words, his reactions, his observations. I took pieces of work, sketches, to him, much as a doggy runs to his owner with a dirty stick for approval, for strokes. I needed stroking. I took a family tree to him so that he could disentangle my reminiscences when they so rarely came.

I've not yet mentioned grief, or mourning, or sorrow, or remorse. After the initial shock and self-revulsion I knew I had no right to grieve or mourn, however much I wanted to. Grief was for the innocent, and that I was not. I felt as the days went on that the pain inside me was growing stronger, larger, feeding upon the well of guilt, the turmoil of horror and repulsion, the tumult of questions and uneasiness that rose and gushed inside the unquiet me. I rarely cried outside the doctor's office, yet when I was in there not a sound passed from me as tears dripped down my face. It seemed an admission of weakness to cry noisily; I felt I would be easing myself too much if I did so. I understood nothing sometimes, then at other times I was filled almost by surprise with a huge well of disgust and comprehension that was gone from me before I managed to harness it.

I had been in Holloway only three weeks before I was due to appear in the magistrates' court in Towcester in Northamptonshire for another remand. Roy called at the prison and handed me a piece of paper listing the reasons why, at the last hearing, bail had been refused. 'For the accused's own protection and welfare she will be remanded into custody for twenty-one days. The prosecution are concerned that she will attempt to take her own life.' He had reached an understanding with the police that until a suitable place was found for me – a psychiatric hospital – for tests and for assessment, I would stay in Holloway.

The van left the prison with me and three officers 'just in case' I tried to do anything silly (the last thing on my mind). We passed through desolate, littered Archway and houseproud Golders Green, then out through Mill Hill and suburban Finchley. When we arrived, I found myself yawning helplessly. I had been woken from my drugged sleep, patchy but deep, at 5a.m. and had not left the nick until 8.30. Alan's mother was there, and my uncle and two aunts. Detectives sat stiffly in their cheap blue suits, one with his shirt stretched tightly over his belly, a flicker of white skin showing. They did not wear beige raincoats and trilbies. My lawyer swallowed painfully, pulling at his tie. He spoke to the prosecutor before the magistrates arrived. When they entered, I was prodded by the WPC who stood alongside my dock seat and told to stand. I thought of school, and the headmaster's visit to the classrooms where we all had to rise as he entered. This was, we were told, a sign of respect for our elders and betters. Nothing had changed. And neither had anything altered in my circumstances – I was discussed by my lawyer and the police prosecutor as if I were truly not present. I learnt much later on that this was probably more likely to happen to women than to men: to be treated as if I were not capable of my own defence and my own personal responsibility.

They decided that I was better off where I was 'for the time being', and all returned hastily to their country cottages while I returned to jail. My eyes bore into Roy's back, the silent question being 'How long for?' I had no appreciation of time, but wanted to know how long I would be in Holloway, how long until I went to a hospital, how long until 'they' decided what to do with me. No answers came, but then my questions were silent.

Back at my home in Holloway, Marlene awaited me. 'What was it like? What did they say?' 'They' was our collective word for all those in any position of authority over us, which at that time constituted about 93 per cent of the population in our vicinity.

I told her all, and that I was to go back yet again in three weeks. She sat on the edge of the bed, so tiny that she could easily swing her legs, and stared unhappily at me, chewing her lip. She was awaiting the judgement of the courts, and the ever-present looming fear of hospitalization.

I had my visitors to fill up my days, (Alan's mother, Ken and Jo, and other relatives), and letters by the bundle. Nothing much had hit the press, so only very few people knew. They had all written to me and continued to correspond, regardless of the fact that I did not reply. I dreaded visits. I had nothing to say that was constructive or valuable, and I usually fought to hold back dry and painful tears. People wanted explanations which I could not give. They desperately needed reassurances, to know that it was all a terrible mistake or some physical malfunction of my brain. These reassurances I could not give either. So I said little, and they talked all the more to fill up the silence. Alan came back from Northern Ireland; he occasionally wrote letters, very brief ones, and more often sent cards.

He came, eventually, to see me. I went to him in the visiting room, unsure of his reaction. It was the first time since it happened that I had seen him. We stared at each other, then he stared at the table, tracing with his stubby fingers the many marks and cigarette burns carved there. I sat miserably, wanting to speak of important things, of love, and of the son that he did not know he had; instead, both grateful for the other's cowardice, we talked of how bad the prison food was, and of his mother's health, and many other things, evading the decisions that had to be made. He came again, and I dithered each time, wanting to be honest, at last, to tell him of his child, dully putting off the evil moment in fear of his reaction.

Roy came; he didn't believe my story about the rape, and pleaded with me to tell him the truth. Listlessly, I insisted that *was* the truth, and carried on with the transparent fabrication I had so desperately invented. A psychiatrist came to give me an interview – an interrogation by any other name. I felt nothing as I trotted out the half-truths, and cold shame as I paraded the lies. He saw at once through the weak tissue of my story, and tried to persuade me that I would help myself if I told him what really happened instead of the 'rape'. At that stage I still wanted to protect Alan from being dragged into the case; I wanted him to be unconnected with me and my prospective burdens. Of course all the shrinks knew that I was lying, but they had no recourse except to see this as an example of my manipulative or mad nature, depending on which viewpoint they favoured.

But Alan kept on coming, as regularly as he could, perhaps feeling in some obscure and oddly perceptive way that he had more to blame himself for than he at first realized. There came a day when I felt that I should let him know about Alex, and so I told him, as gently and yet as firmly as I could. He cried. He had never done so before, not being given to displays of any sort of emotion. I felt embarrassed, and wished for a hole in the ground to immerse myself in, or sackcloth and ashes, or possibly both. It had both hurt and touched him to know that he had a child, a boy child, and he made rash and excited promises that he would leave the army when his contract was up, and we would find a little house, and all three of us would live there together, presumably happily-ever-after. I watched him as he described the patterns of things to come, blindly and subconsciously omitting the realities that I was in jail, and likely to be there for some time, awaiting some kind of judgement; that I no longer had legal custody of my son; that I had no home, no money and no future. That was how it was. I kept my feelings about Alex completely separate from Alan's plans. It was never going to happen so better not waste time wishing or thinking.

The blind leading the blind, I nodded and encouraged and listened as he told me of his plans. I watched, and I did not like what it was that I saw, but it was familiar, and the old devil in me stuck with the little in my life that was constant. I did not disillusion him, feeling with a certain knowledge that none of his half-baked ideas would ever come near fruition. Instead I felt that it was better to nod and encourage and nurture his naîvety in the kindest way possible. Finally we both ran out of things to say, and luckily visiting time was halted by a screw. The other women longed for the extended visits which I got, because of the distance my people came, but I would gladly have traded with them. Exhausted with restraining my emotions, I went back to the safety of the wing where the screams of the women and the banging of chairs upon doors and heads upon walls drowned out the thoughts that occupied my head.

Out of the blue came the news that my mother's funeral was about to be held – the body had been released, said the psychiatrist who broke the news to me. I was left alone to digest this information. I had the choice to go if I wanted to, accompanied by two officers. All the family and friends had told me that if I wanted to go, and felt that it would not upset me too much, I must go, and that they would be happy with whatever decision I made. They felt it was right that I should attend. I knew I had to go, whatever it would do to me afterwards. It was tradition, and Catholic tradition at that, and I was not brave or foolish enough to deviate from my childhood pattern of obeying the unwritten rules of Church etiquette.

It was a beautiful day; instead of the blustery cold and freezing wind that had blown over my father's body, the sun shone with an August softness. The two officers sent with me reassured me that it would be all right: they would be there, and they had, they assured me earnestly, plentiful supplies of tissues with them. 'Seen 'em like you, before, I have,' said one, short and plump, sweet-faced.

'Poor love... if it gets too bad, just you grab hold of my hand. Eee – isn't she pale, Ann?' This remark came from the other officer, a Newcastle woman of Amazonian proportions, bony of body and husky-voiced.

I had been told by a senior officer that to make things easier for me and my family the transport would be an unmarked car, a taxi, and the officers would wear plain clothes. This was not to be. Somewhere there had been a hitch in the proceedings, and the result was a huge van with bars at all windows, and the words 'HM Prison' all over the side. No one at the funeral could have been unaware of where I had come from. It made no difference to me, but I felt it might be embarrassing for the congregation. As it happened, everyone was too nervous and worried about my possible mental state to care about how I and the prison's representatives appeared.

The church seemed beautiful, even to me, scornful as I was of Catholic ritual. So was the service, had I been sufficiently in one piece to hear it properly. I sat stiff, upright, unmoved, until, to my shock, the coffin was wheeled in and deposited almost next to me. On either side of me sat Little and Large of Holloway. I grabbed, as instructed, and found a warm and comforting hand enclose mine. Tissues were pressed into my other hand, and I tried to mop up the flood. I still made no noise, but let the gates open a little.

I had been forced back into the living world, ironically, by a sudden and brutal confrontation with death. I felt then, as I had not done before, that it must have really happened, that she must be dead, and here was her body. I could not take in properly the idea that my mother, who had been the only person constantly around me, despite the fact that I had never known her without barriers, now lay cold in a coffin. Coffins were for dead people, and so she must be dead. I became very rational in my desperation and calmed down momentarily until the priest, our old, familiar, family priest, began to sing a hymn she had loved. That was it. I felt the pain as fresh as before I blocked it out on the night that I killed her. Reality came back, numbness left me, mercilessly, and I was back in the world of pain and death and loss and grief, with no safety blanket there to shield me from the evidence.

It was a sharp, fresh-bleeding wound. I had not realized how deeply it was possible to suffer until then, and even so I knew that I still did not have the right to grieve, to suffer, to keen. I saw again the imprint, as a negative, of blood on my hands, and felt that no pain was too great for me to bear, no punishment enough. Resolutely, I decided to make the years of life left to me as hard and as pain-filled as they could possibly be. Whatever 'they' in charge of my welfare might decide, I would now scourge myself in every way that I could.

The funeral ended. The graveside ceremony was as horrific and unreal as it had been seven years earlier when my other parent had been buried. The afternoon had turned cold. People shivered, wanting to be gone, unsure of what to say to me. For how do you commiserate with a murderess? How could they say to me that they were sorry about my loss, and press my hand uneasily? Instead I was given wintry kisses and mumbled sentences, and was then thankfully led away by my two not insensitive minders.

Back at the nick I felt a pressure gone, the pressure of how to feel about myself when I could not even acknowledge what I had actually done. I could not speak of it to Roy, when he came to try to prepare a report for the court to ask for some sort of bail. Now I knew how I felt, and what my way should be. Brought up in the vein of self-reprimand, and with the thread of guilt thinly skimming my every move, it came as second nature to me now to slip back into the frame of mind that Anna was bad, and Anna must punish herself accordingly. Roy insisted that I must co-operate with the specialists who came to see me; in his letters he stressed, 'It is very important that you co-operate with Dr T―― ' as he might be very helpful in obtaining your transfer from Holloway Prison to a hospital. Please do everything you can to be honest and straightforward – this is not the time to judge yourself.' At that point no one was at all sure what was going to happen to me. The experts whose job it was to diagnose me were undecided too. It was early days to make an assessment, and so I was seen by three more doctors in the quest for an analysis that they all agreed upon sufficiently to decide whether I was mad or merely bad.

On the advice of the prison doctor I started to keep a diary, though I showed it to nobody. It seemed to ease me a little to be able to write what I felt without the fear of interpretation. On no account could I give voice to these things without fear of facing the nightmare of my own despair.

28 August 1986. 3p.m. Time for contemplation. What else can you do in prison but think? Everything hurts. I want to get it all down, somehow contain the pain. Tears are no good any more. I can't yet go to the edge of the pain that I sense lies in waiting for me . . . only feel my way round it, not nearly enough. I feel blind, searching my way towards some kind of comprehension but this evades me . . . the flashbacks are worse, they are for always. The nightmares are parallel to the snatches of memory in the daylight. I used to think that the nightmares only came when it was dark, but they can live in the sun . . . .

More doctors, more diagnoses. I saw one, who was deputy head of medical services in the prison, for ten minutes. He spoke to me about the problems I had with my periods, which were still like haemorrhages every month. I regarded them as no more than a phase of my self-flagellation – little and often. I soon discovered that small doses of self-inflicted pain or endurance hurt more than the pain I imagined must have been caused by the head-banging of some women on the wing – like water torture. I slept more easily at night for the daily bout of exquisitely fine measures of punishment.

After three months in Holloway, I was told of the result of the continuous stream of doctors. Roy was going to ask the court to allow me to be bailed to the secure unit of a mental hospital in Northampton, partly for reports and partly, as Roy subsequently said in court, to get me away from the 'terrible conditions and appalling influence of Holloway and its inhabitants'.

Before I made my three-weekly appearance at the magistrates' court in Towcester I begged Roy to let me stay in Holloway a while longer. I felt safe there, I tried to explain. I felt that on the wing, mad and chaotic and worrying though it might all be, I had friends. I knew that prison was where I should be.

Roy looked despairing. He explained steadily and patiently to me, as one might to a child or a drunkard, what he would say in court, and how he thought the magistrates would react. He was, he said worriedly, not hopeful that they would let me go anyway because of the reasons given previously. He would do his best, he said, and I was not to get upset, or angry, or rude, if they said no. I wondered if I should have worn pigtails and ankle socks or tried sucking my thumb, and generally behave like a small spoilt child, since that was how it seemed that I was perceived – that I must have my own way, and if not I would stamp my feet upon the ground imperiously.

The court sat, and the accused rose. Up and down we went for the convention of the court procedure. Roy spoke to Their Honours about the trauma of Holloway Prison on such a young, vulnerable girl, still only a teenager, thrown into a place full of madwomen and child sex-perverts, trans-sexuals and lesbians. The Bench looked sympathetic. They had seen me before them so many times by now that I almost wanted to wave hello to them. They eyed me indulgently, spoke sharply to the police spokesperson about any intentions they might have about opposing this application, and granted bail there and then on the conditions already outlined by Roy. The Bench smiled at me and called me Miss Reynolds. I was now a Miss because I was no longer a prisoner.

The court was dismissed, and the lawyers fluttered away. This time I was taken out through the front door. I was given a chair to sit on at the entrance like an old Italian lady, to observe all that passes her door. The chair even had a cushion. What a difference bail makes.

Chapter Seven

I walked on to the ward still accompanied by the keepers of the law. It was a large, open-plan room with huge sashed windows that I could actually see out of. There was a pool table with a young guy standing playing at it; and a nursing station, the point of observation. We stood rather stupidly, unsure of what to do next. A fat man who I guessed was probably a patient came up to us and asked us in a strong Glaswegian voice what we wanted. We looked at each other doubtfully. The pool player, this man told us, was actually a patient – 'but not representative of the general rabble here' – he himself was the charge nurse who reigned over the ward. He seemed to relish giving this morsel of information. He told me in a loud but strangely confidential whisper that he did not feel that I was to be treated like a patient, someone with a mental illness, but that I was to be watched carefully at all times. . . .

Then they told me, as more staff appeared to break the silence between us, that I was the only woman on the ward, and that it had been *ages* since they had had any women there. The men would just have to adjust to me, they said, and I to them.

Then they led me to a little, womblike room with an immensely high ceiling and two lots of wooden shutters on the inside of the cavernous window. This was to stop me from jumping out and killing myself or escaping. It also prevented me from getting the air and views I so craved. The door had a window in it, controlled with blinds from outside so that I could be seen but not see. Great. A door on the window and a window in the door. I wanted out already, and I had hardly set foot in the place.

Once again my few possessions were checked and I was variously allowed and disallowed articles. I was given bedding and left to make up the bed. So what had changed? And was anything *supposed* to have changed? Why had I thought that things would be different, better, now that I was no longer in prison?

In those first few weeks I longed so desperately and painfully for Holloway that it was a constant and unrelieved ache inside of me. My new role was unclear. Previously I had been a prisoner, and only that. Here I was technically not a prisoner, yet clearly imprisoned. I was someone to be watched over. For some reason I felt immensely depressed and unable to do anything except sit and cry.

The atmosphere did not help my mood. Ten men and I shared the confines of the ward where eating, sleeping and other activities took place. The men were nearly all sex attackers of one form or another – old women, little children or just plain old rape. Most of them had spent a long time in one of the secure hospitals, Broadmoor or Rampton. They were persistent offenders and totally institutionalized. Two of them used to masturbate often throughout the day and evening, sitting in the armchairs near the TV, close to the entrance to the ward. The staff thought, on the whole, that they were harmlessly amusing and gently chastised them.

Every day, games were played on the ward. The chairs and tables were pushed back and a ball produced from the office. The game itself was indefinable, a sort of rugby-cum-soccer where I, as the only woman apart from the nurses – who didn't really count as they wore the uniform of 'Don't touch me' starched dresses and unbecoming hats – was the object of more contact than the ball. 'Don't forget, you're the first young female they've seen this side of the ward for years,' explained one male member of staff reassuringly. Oh. Well. Of course. That made me feel ever so much better.

After a while, I tearfully started to refuse to join in these games. I was told by the charge nurse that I was not going to be allowed to disturb his ward routine. He ordered me out of the room that I now tried to hide in all day, and told me that if I did not join in the games, and start eating and drinking properly – I had begun to refuse food, not having a great deal of appetite – he would see to it that the court ordered me to stay in the hospital as long as they wanted. This was always possible, I knew, and I thought twice about being 'disobedient'. So I capitulated and joined in the games occasionally, and also took food from the proffered trolley, surreptitiously feeding the nearby plants with the gruesome stuff. I took to eating apples whenever the charge nurse was around, and took full advantage of my period pains, which seemed to last an awful long time, to excuse myself from the games.

After a while like this, Roy, who was as horrified by the ward as I was, applied to the court for the conditions of bail to be changed so that I could go to an open ward where the patients were less extreme. The court agreed, and I went back to the hospital hopeful of release from the Ward of Horrors. But it was not to be. The consultant on the open ward said that he would not take the responsibility of having a suicide risk on his ward. His was a ward full of people with dead eyes, who looked exhausted by life itself: people pale, thin, blank, for whom the business of getting through each day had become too much. They had broken down, like an old and weary car, and it was with them that I felt I belonged.

Christmas came, and with it Alan. He was peculiarly evasive, speaking little, and studiously avoided touching me. Obviously he was highly embarrassed about the whole thing, and I wondered bitterly which he was more ashamed of – visiting me in prison, or the stigma of the mental hospital. He reiterated his former promises, weaker now, of a little flat somewhere, us, our son. I tried to tell him gently that it would not happen, any of it, that nothing would ever again be that simple, that clear-cut, but he would not listen. It was as if he had programmed himself to listen only to what he wanted to hear, and to tune the rest out. I sighed, and tried to tell him, as I had told myself, that there were, as Roy told me, 'a range of options for the judge to consider when he gives sentence, and you must be aware of this, from probation to a life sentence'. But Alan talked almost feverishly of his own plans and ridiculous ideas, and denied that it might be impossible to wipe things as clean as he seemed to think they could be. I saw with slicingly painful clarity that he could not cope with the reality of prison for life for me, or see how it would affect him. It was not something he was prepared even to consider.

But it was something to which I myself was coming closer and closer with every passing day. I willed it to happen. I wanted nothing more than prison, the blessed relief of judgement. I just waited for the words to be uttered. On 19 December I wrote in my diary:

> I am so very scared, so terrified. I seem to have no control over myself and my leaky emotions at the moment. My punishment must be to bear this period of intolerable suspense. All the things I have ever dealt with in my life seem like a trail of events which hardly touched me on the outside but have left their indefinable mark inside me. My soul must have many leaks in the seam. I have worked it out now. I am ready to start a prison sentence, it's right that I should.

I did not let myself think about Alan, though there were times when, unasked, those thoughts crept in and assailed me anyway. I still had visits from the social worker, less and less frequently, and these I had to prepare myself for, steeling myself against the thoughts which her careless words touched off in me. Some days I felt strong, and resolutely able to face whatever came, but on others I felt as if it had all wearied me too much, and that my life blood was draining away. My trial had been set for mid-February, and I did not know if I would be able to cope.

> I have to have some reserves of strength left for the trial. There are two ways to handle it. Either I can try to be strong and get through it all and then collapse

when I get to the relative sanctity of Holloway. Or I can relinquish all efforts to stay sane and together and collapse before the trial. If this happens it will finish me.

I spent a lot of time in the little room with the shuttered window, huddled into a corner, tearing at myself with my thoughts. I imagined a room which was bare, with no window and a locked door, where I could howl and scream and wrench my grief from me in peace and loneliness, with no one to hear or worry or chastise me for my noise – no one to suppose that it was for show, or for the benefit of the doctor's reports, or for the court, or to get medicine. With a fervour that made me restless, I longed for that space.

I'm eighteen still. Can this be possible? I have great fundamental doubts about my life, about its need to continue. I don't have anything left to cry for, so why am I? I've lost it all, by my own hands. Am I evil? I don't want to think so, but I must be. From now on I will be stronger, and accept whatever happens as no less than the least that I deserve.

In January 1987 I was introduced to the barristers who were to act for me at the trial. They told me that the judge would not accept the plea of 'guilty to manslaughter but not guilty to murder' which Roy had advised me to make, and that there would still be a full trial. I listened dully. It did not matter to me. The only reason for pleading not guilty to murder had been so that there could be a trial – a trial would cause me pain and agony, and I wanted revenge upon myself.

The consultant for the ward I was on interviewed me for a report to the court on my state of mind then and previously. The interview was recorded on video, to be used in a training exercise for students.

It was getting very near to the approximate date of the trial when the ward erupted. There were then two other women besides me, for a change; one middle-aged, confused and disorientated, who apparently had an annual breakdown in much the same way that most of us have a holiday, and an eighty-year-old widow whose daughter had just killed herself. She herself was thought to be a suicide risk through shock and grief, and had been moved on to the secure ward 'just in case'. The more women on the ward, the more the tension increased. One morning I was told by a gossipy member of staff that two new men were detectives who had come to investigate an alleged rape of the younger woman.

The night staff, who often slept on duty anyway, had not noticed anything until the bemused and terrified woman had come and told them what had happened. The alleged rapist was a huge ex-boxer who weighed about twenty-two stone, a frighteningly childlike man who did not know his own strength and had hands like huge steaks. He watched everything that took place on the ward with a calculating, sly look. At about ten o'clock at night he had apparently followed the woman up the corridor which led away from the main area. She had gone into the men's loos by mistake – this being quite easy to do both because there were no signs on the doors to indicate male or female, and because the men were so unused to having any women on the ward that they used both loos anyway. This resulted in complete confusion for both sexes especially for those who were confused and disorientated to start with. He had followed her in and then, she said, raped her.

He was a man who did not seem to have any sense of right or wrong; when he wanted something, he saw no reason why he should not have it. This may well have applied that night. The woman was not a compulsive liar or suffering from delusions, so there was little reason why she should lie. Anyway, the detectives came in to sort it all out and stayed for a long time, questioning us all as to whether we had seen anything.

The accused man was removed from his bed in the open-plan ward and, like a huge, silent horse, locked into a cell with stable doors at the end of the ward. This cell was visible immediately you came on to the ward. His head could be seen straining to see over the stable door and the pounding of his feet could be heard as he walked on the spot all day, all night – a legacy of his boxing days, he told us. The staff began to feel sorry for him and took to sending him double portions of food at mealtimes. He demolished it all, hardly stopping to chew, and continued to pace like a headless chicken. We were never told whether he had actually raped her. He was kept locked up for nearly two months, after which he was to be transferred to Rampton.

After that little incident, I felt unsafe on the ward. I had never particularly trusted the staff. Now I felt that their attitudes had been blasé and callous towards the incident and its potential repercussions for the already ill victim, never mind about the aggressor.

I thought a lot in those days about what it was that had led me to the point I had reached in my life. As a substitute for therapy I wrote everything down:

> It's true that since Dad died I've hunted desperately for a substitute, a father figure, in all the men I've met... men – I mean boys. Little boys. The only way to replace him without dislodging the memories of him was to find a lover with the same qualities as Dad... surely that's not so odd, is it? The only problem is that I had to sleep with the substitutes because even I couldn't expect them to be platonic.

It had taken me all that time to come to terms with my feelings about my father's death. I realized then, in that intense period of self-reflection, that grief delayed is grief multiplied – it doesn't go away simply because you sit on it and refuse to admit it into your life. I was mourning the death of my Daddy seven years too late.

I tried a little now to immerse myself in hospital life. Just before the trial Alan came up and found me sitting with one of the other patients, teaching him poker. 'A year ago, even a few months ago, you wouldn't have sat at the same table as him, much less played cards with him,' he said, miffed to see that I did not appear overwhelmed at his sudden reappearance. I was starting to discover just how small a part he played in my thoughts these days. On the advice of the ward GP, I even went to relaxation classes and wrote about them in my diary:

> I am very tense and have trouble breathing properly because of this, so he suggests that I go to these classes held in a hut in the grounds of the hospital. The nurse will gladly take me, he says. She does not look glad to be taking me. She is a large, Cindy doll-like figure who seems to be much, much taller than me. Maybe this is my sense of inferiority getting the better of me. We sit waiting for the instructor. It is February, and bloody freezing. The instructor arrives, a young, thin man with an angry rash of pimples around his neck. He eyes us and explains that other patients will also be coming. My nurse smiles and introduces herself. He looks at her with a mixture of admiration and awe. I can see him thinking: 'A fine figure of a woman.' Perhaps they will get together.
>
> The others arrive. One is a splendid large lady, dark-eyed, who wears a floral pinny as if she has come to double up as the tea lady. The other is a small man who looks even more nervous than the instructor. We are told to lie down on the floor and some very bad music is played, with plenty of crashing crescendos and similar unrelaxing things. We are asked if we feel relaxed. Everyone looks at everyone else. The small man asks if he can relieve himself. The instructor flushes at this need of the weak flesh. Once the man returns, we are told to loosen each part of our body, and the man once more announces that, because he is loosened, he now needs to pee again. The instructor grimaces and says that will be all for today. Are we all relaxed? He hopes so. He looks anything but relaxed to me.

As the winter crept by, I was insulated from the worst of the weather. Occasionally the staff allowed me to go for a walk in the grounds or to the little village with a couple of members of staff. These ventures were curiously painful. I noticed everything with the bittersweet strangeness of nostalgia and regret. The bare trees and the frost-smeared grounds seemed poignantly beautiful to me then, knowing how long it would be before I was to see them again.

The day set for the plea hearing came nearer, and arrangements were made by the hospital to escort me to the court in Northampton. The relaxation nurse was the lucky one. She had no interest in the affair – but then, I reflected, it wasn't her life that was about to be sliced up and thrown to the legal lions.

The day dawned. I don't remember what the weather was like. I just remember thinking, 'At last I can get away from this awful place' and, hypocritically, 'Please, God, don't let them send me back here.' After we arrived at the court – an old building designed to intimidate, or so it seemed – we sat for ages in the foyer until the defence 'team' arrived, bewigged and begowned. In we filed. The court room itself was cold, with tall ceilings and a long, thin window, wide open.

As I sat in the dock I listened to the two versions as the two sides presented them, blanking out what I could. I had already seen all the statements and depositions by all the people involved, so none of that part came as a surprise. I had primed myself over and over to be as calm and as controlled as possible when the facts of that night were read out. The clerk of the court motioned to me to stand. I was asked how I intended to plead. 'Guilty,' I said, without really thinking of anything except the horror of what was to come. Roy gestured to me furiously. I amended my plea to 'guilty to manslaughter but not guilty to murder', the charge against me. The press scribbled frantically. Up until then they had not known what my plea would be. Neither had I. . . .

The judge and my lawyer discussed the matter of a trial – for trial it was clear there would be. The question now was when. The court was not free at the moment for a trial, the judge said. 'I think, in fact,' said he, 'that there are no slots until the end of April at the earliest.'

This was the end. I knew with utter certainty that I

could not stay three more months on that ward in a sane state of mind. Roy saw the set of my face.

Later, back at the hospital, I drowned in waves of self-pity. How much longer? The anti-climax was unbearably frustrating. I wandered the ward, restless to the pitch where I wanted to scream and stamp my feet. With venom in my voice I refused to play the hospital games. The staff sensed they should not try to aggravate me now, and left me alone. The next day Roy, the miracle worker, rang. The judge had decided that he could fit me in on the following Monday for a week. I was delighted to get this news. The staff, not knowing how I felt, held their collective breath, fearing tears and remonstrations from me. Not bloody likely.

Now the staff went on paranoia overdrive. Worried that I might try to kill myself due to the pressure that would be around me, they stepped up their watchfulness and never let me out of their sight for a second. If I lingered in the bathroom for more than a minute, they pounded on the door in alarm; then, should I not answer due for instance to the noise of running water, they rushed in in panic. Everything that could possibly be construed as a suicidal tool was taken out of my room. Then they took everything else 'just in case'. They asked me to give them all my clothes and wear my night things instead. They would give me back my clothes, they said, when I needed to go to court, and only then. I did not quite understand what harm I could do to myself with a T-shirt and a pair of leggings that I couldn't do with a nightshirt, but I was too worn out with fearful anticipation to want to argue.

I was not allowed to enter my room until about eleven o'clock at night; the door was locked until then in case I should go in and try to hang myself. After eleven o'clock, they supposed, a magical change would take place and I would be unlikely to want to kill myself until about seven the following morning. Whenever I needed the loo I had to ask a member of staff, always male, who would stand right outside until, red-faced, I came out again. The men's eyes popped alarmingly at my night attire, which was just about thigh-length. They could not believe their luck. They wanked as usual, but I felt twenty times more vulnerable.

Bathtime was fun, too. After running the thing, if I was in there for more than five minutes a member of staff would enter to check on me. The (male) patients wandered in, too, having made 'a mistake' and 'accidentally' opened the wrong door. Really? Three times in a night? One or two male members of staff made the same 'mistake' too. Perhaps they too thought that I had been trying to drown myself in the two inches of bathwater that I was allowed.

Sunday evening, my last day of 'freedom' before the trial, passed in a very low-key way, the ward its usual noisy, chaotic, unpleasant, tense self. I tried to not get tense myself, conserving my mental energies for the morrow. It was not that easy.

Monday morning came, and I dressed very ordinarily, not seeing the point in trying to begin to make any kind of illusory impression. This time I had been assigned a different nurse, one with an air of professional detachment. She wore no uniform, and we rode to the court house in a taxi. I watched in the foyer as the place filled up with an assortment of defendants and their entourage. Most of my family turned up, together with assorted friends and supporters – much against my will. In vain I had asked them all not to attend.

I was summoned into a little room by my lawyer for a 'chat' with the barristers. They advised me on demeanour, and advised me strongly against going into the witness box myself and being cross-examined, which they said would prejudice the case strongly and unfairly against me.

'Then I shall,' I said to them. I wanted it to be as painful as possible.

The lawyers looked wearily despairing already. They wondered, no doubt, why I was wasting their time when I could have pleaded guilty and got it all over with. I felt no need to give explanations. They would be more than adequately paid for their time by the state, and the longer the trial took, the more they got. The only thing that mattered to them, they told me, was my welfare and that I must on no account be so cynical – it would look bad in court, precocious.

What difference did it make to me what it looked like? They could never understand that I wanted the worst, not the easiest, and that I wanted to go the longest way round to that goal.

We were ushered into the court. It was as before, family and friends behind me, press alongside me. When the court room was full, the clerk flung open the little door leading to the judge's chambers and said, 'Court rise.' We all did. Judgement Day was here.

Chapter Eight

After all the expectation and the nerves, the actual beginning of the trial was a trifle anti-climactic. The court room was too cold, said the prosecution. The defence agreed. The judge, Mr Justice Tudor-Evans, decreed that the windows be closed and the heating turned on. It was, after all, he said, February. Everybody nodded. The judge was terribly old, and very small and wrinkled, like an ancient crumbly garden gnome, only not as funny. He found hearing difficult, it seemed, and his half-glasses kept slipping off his small red nose. I felt that this was not a good start.

I was not sure where to look or what to do with myself. I peered behind me, and saw my supporters nervously motioning to me to turn back and face the judge. The press peered up at me, and I down at them. One reporter had wild, myopic eyes and hair poking out of his ears. I turned away.

I looked at the judge and then at the jurors, who stared hungrily back at me, devouring the defendant. I did not want my gaze to dwell on them so I turned my attention to the lawyers and stared instead at the backs of their wigs. Dirty. Grey where white should have been. It helped to focus on something so absurd and archaic. My barrister's wig was perfectly groomed, as affluent-looking as he himself. The prosecutor had a grimy slip of a wig perched rather precariously on top of his narrow head. I darted a glance at the judge again and met his eye, learning in the process what the word 'baleful' meant. He seemed to peer at me with a great deal of interest, but that may well have been because he could not really see me properly.

The actual mechanics of the first morning in court passed fairly easily for me, with a summary introduction by both sides and the judge's words to the jury. When, with a relieved look from the judge, we retired for lunch, I was led down to the cells underneath the court room. Northampton is an old court and it has not changed with the years. I was led to a tiny cell hot with claustrophobia. As soon as I was inside the gates swung to, and the nurse outside stood looking slightly guiltily at me through the bars of my little cage. There was no air or light in that little box within a box within a box . . . the floor was filthy, and the only furniture was yet another bloody wooden bench. I'd almost forgotten life without them. I did start to panic a little, closed in alone with my tears and grief, but it soon occured to me that I ain't seen nothin' yet, so I'd better not get too low yet.

The afternoon was spent listening, or in my case deliberately not listening, to the forensic scientist expounding theories of a more technical nature. My head spun with the effort, and after I realized he had stopped talking I felt the pain and the dull throbbing of an incipient headache. I frowned, trying to will it away before the pain intensified. The talk started again. I dimmed it out to a low drone, meaningless except for the hum and whirr of my unsuppressible imagination. The tears were unstoppable too, though silent, and I felt the migraine settle over me like a vulture waiting to pick at what would be left after the first day at court.

At last the judge announced that the court would resume the next day at ten. We all rose and I was left alone until everyone else had departed, with regretful looks at me. Too tired to stir my limbs, I could not move. The nurse came up to me and laid her hand on my shoulder, surprised to see me flinch. More than anything I did not want to be touched. We waited in the empty, littered foyer for the taxi.

The prosecutor passed us and stopped beside me, bending down. We eyed each other and I waited for him to speak. It came drily, in clipped public school tones. 'There's a horde of press photographers waiting for you. There's a back way out if you want. I'll show you . . . . ' I turned to the nurse. She felt that we should avoid them, but I knew with some little experience that they would only pursue us on one of the other days, and I would be in progressively worse shape as the week wore on. Better to face them now than later. So out we walked. I kept my head down, and said nothing. Flashes flashed, questions were asked, mikes appeared. I climbed into the taxi with the nurse and off we sped, two lone hacks chasing us down the road a little just for the sake of it. My eyes were still blinded from the flashes.

On 9 February I wrote in my diary:

> Back at the hospital, I take off my 'provocative' nightie (that's what the staff have labelled it, as a great joke. They don't have to sit here wearing it, do they?). It sits oddly upon me with my mask of exhaustion. I am like a child. I have no wish but to be loved, comforted, cuddled, held, cared for. Yet I know none of those things are mine anyway, never have been, never will be, certainly. Who cares? I don't. I want to sleep and wake up and it all be different – clean, and not pain-filled. I am so scared that I can hardly think. I am paralysed with fright about the next four days . . . . I can't remember when it last didn't hurt so much that tears were just on the edge of everything. Every movement inside my mind stings me. Why won't they let me go to bed? They are cruel jailers. I have in my mind that I have another four days at least like this one. I put my head down and lie there in the almost complete darkness. Every now and then the blessed dark is broken by one of the patients coming to peer in at the window on the door. Or the nurse, to check on me . . . . Why won't they let me sleep?

Those next four days went by in a similar haze of waking and sleeping, pain and more pain. On one day the medical experts were called to give their evidence. There were five of them, but only three were present in the court, my lawyers having decided that the other two who had written reports would only confuse the court. I did not see these reports until long after the trial.

The police surgeon who had seen me when I was first brought into the station gave his evidence. He felt that I was certainly suffering from depression, possibly post-natal, and was very much 'on my side'. Then the Holloway doctor took his place on the stand. He had not interviewed me himself; his report was based on those of the other doctors and on conversations with a psychiatrist whom I had seen when I was about thirteen. 'She has a premorbid personality with marked histrionic traits,' he said. 'I feel that the issue of the defendant's responsibility for her actions or omissions at the time should be put before a jury.' Dr Hindson, who made these comments, was the senior medical officer at Holloway. When Dr O'Connor, the Holloway doctor who had seen the most of me, was cross-examined, he was asked, 'Is the principal medical officer at Holloway a qualified psychiatrist?'

'No,' he answered.

The judge intervened: 'That is Dr Speed?'

'Yes,' replied Dr O'Connor.

He was then asked by counsel: 'Are *you* a qualified psychiatrist?'

'Yes.'

Counsel then asked: 'What about the senior medical officer, Dr Hindson?'

'He is also not a qualified psychiatrist,' Dr O'Connor replied.

Dr O'Connor himself was questioned and cross-questioned about his many interviews with me and the assumptions he had drawn from them. He made, I think, a good impression at the beginning. He was reasonable, softly but clearly spoken, and dressed conservatively; he displayed no alarmingly strange traits to make the jurors label him a typical mad shrink. He spoke of how he had seen me on more than twenty occasions over two and a half months, each interview lasting around an hour and a half. In addition he had talked to Alan and to the social worker involved with the adoption, and had discussed my case with the other psychiatrists involved.

He talked of how, for the first couple of weeks, 'Anna seemed to be cut off from her surroundings in some way. She was emotionally numbed. After the initial period of detachment and objectivity, as if she were talking about someone else, she began to show signs of great distress and depression: feelings of hopelessness and guilt that evidently went back many years.' He went on to say that 'In my opinion, at the material time she was suffering from such abnormality of mind induced by disease, namely depression, as substantially impaired her mental responsibility for the acts in doing the killing within the meaning of the Homicide Act.'

My counsel asked Dr O'Connor if he was in any way partial to the matter.

His answer was: 'My original report was prepared for the prosecution, in the first place.'

He talked about the effects that the concealed pregnancy would have had upon my personality. 'I feel they would have had a very serious and prolonged adverse effect on a young woman's mental state. She was very young while going through what is for most women a very difficult period. She had no support from her mother because she had chosen to conceal the pregnancy, and she chose to try and get through this very difficult period by herself. I feel that this must have put her under an immense amount of strain. Her impairment would have been substantial because of her disease.'

Counsel asked him what he meant by this.

'Depression is classified as a disease by medical people. The difference between normal and clinical depression, however, is a persistent lowering of mood. A depression is qualitatively different from "normal" run-of-the-mill unhappiness, and symptoms include feeling depressed, hopeless, miserable, often suicidal, having sleep disturbances, appetite disturbance and weight loss.' He told the court that when a person has a disease of the mind such as depression their ability to interpret their surroundings or their own life situation is impaired. A person in a depressed state can sometimes feel that it is their duty to relieve someone of suffering, whereas if they were not depressed they might say that that was an improper thing to do in particular circumstances. 'Now applying that approach to this case, the defendant has told me and others several times that she wanted to take the burden from her mother; that she wanted to relieve her of her suffering. People who have a disease of the mind sometimes act in some kind of irrational way for which there is no particular reason or explanation.'

Later, Dr O'Connor was cross-examined in depth by the prosecution. There came a point where the prosecutor, David Barker, asked him about something that was in his report:

'Just to take you up on your recommendations as a doctor, is it that she is mentally normal now and if she is convicted of anything she should be put on probation?'

At this point my counsel got to his feet to object. 'Does that have any relevance to what the jury have to consider?'

The judge then re-emphasized this point: 'She could be put on probation?'

Crown counsel replied that that was in the doctor's recommendation, and Dr O'Connor added that his report did indeed contain the view that I should be convicted of manslaughter and put on probation. My counsel then said that he would himself have wanted to mention the matter but had assumed that it would be inadmissible.

The judge asked my lawyer, maddeningly slowly, 'The objection . . . is that the disposal of the case in one particular eventuality is a matter for the court, not the doctor. That is what you are saying?'

Counsel explained that the jury should not be swayed one way or the other by reason of what might happen afterwards.

The judge replied: 'Of course, if it were a relevant question. And I express no opinion because I have not yet heard Mr Barker.' Everyone else had, though, including the jury. 'If it were a relevant question, then the vice to which you have just referred could be cured by my pointing out the functions which I and the jury have.'

Barker then made matters really clear by explaining

helpfully: 'The question really is the confusion on her present mental state, and what the question seeks to do is to underline her present normality because that is what this witness is saying, in effect, and that is why I put the question. She is so normal now that even if she was convicted of manslaughter my recommendation would be that she should be on probation.'

Eventually the judge made his decision. 'I do not think that that is really the way to approach the matter, with all respect.'

Crown counsel, smiling now, answered, 'Then if that is your Lordship's view – '

The judge again: 'I am sure that with your great experience and skill there are other ways of putting questions which may have the same result to that which you are seeking; in other words, you can put the question another way.'

Counsel for the Crown: 'I may come back to it . . . . '

Whatever else the well-intentioned doctor might have said, he had inadvertently sealed my fate when he replied to the question put by Crown counsel. The jury would have to consider that, if they found me guilty of manslaughter, I was able to be given a 'sentence' of probation. They would have been unlikely to know about the full range of sentencing open to the judge anyway, since it was most emphatically not their business to concern themselves with such matters.

On the third day, I think, I was called as a witness. Roy and the barristers were still very much against the idea, but I was determined to go ahead. I felt dull and sluggish that morning; I was not sleeping at night, and the long days at court were exhausting me. But I felt glad that it seemed to be easier the more painful it got.

The counsel for the prosecution was very clever. We both had the same hatred for me, and the same wish for the same result. I cried a lot, and got angry and defensive, and my loyalties were raised fiercely in me, and I prayed for it to end. I thought only of how far I could push myself before I came to the end of my abilities. And the end was decided for me by the barrister, when he decided he had heard enough.

I crawled back to the bench and was led down, down to the little wooden cell and locked in. Thankful. Thankful to be locked away from people. And on the penultimate day, all that was left was the summing-up by each 'side', my frustrated barristers whose hands were tied by their foolish and contrary client, playing with the business of the law. They never understood why I wanted to prolong the process of pain. It was something indefinable even to myself, something I had to do before the whole thing could end, when they would leave me alone and I could then sink into the stupor of one to whom time will mean nothing, ever again. Because I knew it would be like that for me.

But of course, sooner or later the dawn has to come, and sometimes it brings with it fresh hope. For me it brought only affirmation of the reality. I was set to work with a broom and a scrubbing brush; work mandatory for a convicted prisoner. As I swept desultorily, along came the medic, a small, grey man with a bulbous nose. Kind eyes, though. I cried as I moved along the corridor, not sweeping very well. He took me into his office and gave me some daytime sedatives. Valium to start with, he said. I, ignorant of what they were, nodded and shuffled out.

Two days I had been back in Holloway, and it seemed both a lifetime and but a short while. Treacherously I slipped back into the prison routine. I needed discipline – welcomed it, in fact, greedily devouring the regularity and the strictness of mealtimes, worktimes, bedtimes, visits. Slowly, then, slowly, I became absorbed into prison life, seeing it as my complete and only world, my thinking distorted with the disorientation of time.

I now shared a dormitory with three other women, Mona, Lacey and Diane. We rose early, through no choice of our own, although I slept so little it was of no consequence to me. First there was a bang on the huge metal door at 6.30, which was followed by a kick or two and finally a head popping in at the hatch to shout at us. I would have woken at four, and, having tired of lying there motionless, would already have got up and been trying to read.

The days for me consisted mostly of scrubbing and more scrubbing, until the corridors and floors gleamed and I was exhausted. But I would not let myself eat, despite the fact that my stomach ached and I felt dizzy and over-tired. No one forced me to work quite as hard as I did, but it was a sort of purging, this manic scrubbing and polishing and cleaning. It worked for a while, until the relentless need for wearing myself out abated a little through sheer physical exhaustion.

One visitor who was unwelcome was the Guardian Ad Litem, the social worker reporting to the court on my views about the adoption. She came to find out what was happening. I explained about the appeal, and how we were waiting for a date. She seemed sympathetic, understanding. She promised that she would do her best to postpone a hearing until after the appeal, so we would all know more about what my position would be. I felt reassured.

Other visits from family and friends were hellish in the first few months of the sentence. We were entitled to one half-hour visit a month, with a second one as a privilege. Since I was always good, I was allowed two a month. My family could not be fobbed off with little white lies about my rights. They had checked conscientiously about what I was and was not allowed, and insisted on turning up with tear-filled eyes every fortnight, bearing gifts of money, tapes for my Sony Walkman and warm, woolly jumpers to enhance my grim wardrobe.

I dreaded visiting time, all for completely selfish reasons. That sounds ungrateful and horrid, and it was. I wanted to be allowed to opt out of life, to close myself away from reality, and visits simply halted this process. I would sit squirming on the hard chairs, wishing for the time to go faster so that I could slip back into unreality. The visits room was too loud, too noisily real, with parents crying, babies screaming, partners arguing.... I hated the noise and the enforced jollity of the visit and feared that my visitors would be just as unhappy. But still they came.

They noticed that I had become used to the Valium, sinking with the stupor of relief into a welcome haze. I lived for the next dose, and often had to be woken up to take it. One day, during an appointment with the prison probation officer, I clutched at the walls and everything spun away from me. I suddenly and fervently longed for my bed, for sleep. Back on the wing, Mona instructed me to lie down. I obeyed thankfully. As I lay there sunk in sleep, the prison nurse tried to wake me for the next dose. 'Wake up, you have to take this. It's been prescribed for you.' Officers shouted, doors banged, a mad woman screamed and wrecked her cell. I heard nothing. I slept on, oblivious to it all. I woke later, dizzily drugged still, when the room was dark.

And outside the walls of Holloway, my little world, strange things were happening. I received a letter from Roy to say that he had submitted notice of appeal, and he enclosed the grounds of appeal from counsel. I was surprised – I had forgotten all about law and legal things.

> The summing up of the law was a model of fairness and clarity . . . [there is] only one point . . . in the hearing of the matter which disturbs me; the initial exchanges between the leading counsel for the Crown and Dr O'Connor, the only expert witness called by either side. The very first question put to Dr O'Connor in cross-examination was to the effect that if he was correct in his diagnosis and a verdict of guilty of manslaughter by reason of diminished responsibility returned by the jury, then the correct sentence would have to be probation since it was clear from his evidence that Anna had recovered from the clinical depression which she suffered from at the time of the killing. The question was wholly improper in dealing at the very least with a matter with which the jury were not concerned. The object in such a question could only be to discredit the witness in the eyes . . . of the jury. They might have felt that they would not wish to see such a killing go unpunished . . . might have recoiled at the idea of probation being imposed . . . one can imagine the sort of impression that questions of sentence might have in any collective jury's mind, but especially in a jury trying such an important and unusual case. The question could have only caused prejudice and should not have been asked. The learned judge did

not specifically mention to the jury that the matter of sentence was for him alone, either at the time it arose or in the summing up.

This was all old news to me, and I was uninterested anyway, except for a momentary flicker of the old ambivalence. Roy had put in an appeal, and I had left it up to him. My probation officer, Graham, wrote to me: 'Appeals do drag on, don't they? There's a flurry of activity, then apparently nothing. A bit like the quiet and stillness after a blizzard has blown itself out. You don't get any interim reports on appeals; it's just a question of waiting and waiting – unfortunately.'

According to the messengers, my visitors, for some strange reason the local Northamptonshire papers had decided that, after they had called me 'evil' and all sorts of other adjectives, my case now 'revealed the shortcomings of the adversarial nature of the British legal system, its origins in the medieval trial by combat, in which a sometimes emotive verbal battle to convince a jury of a defendant's guilt or innocence takes precedence over a dispassionate search for the truth'. It seemed that now the appeal had been filed, and local people had started to make their outrage (for that was what it later transpired to be) felt, the papers had decided that it was wise to forsake sensationalism and reflect the opinion of their readers.

Graham brought cuttings of the latest letters to these papers from church leaders, teachers at the sixth-form college in Brackley, and people who simply felt that a wrong had been done. It seemed that this had all been started by a law student from Brackley, whose mother had taught at the school and whose father had been headmaster there. The student felt that a miscarriage of justice had occurred. He wrote to Roy telling him this, and then sent a long letter to all the local papers, who printed it along with lengthy editorials supporting it. The student said that he was 'shattered and upset by the jury's verdict ... the decision seems to be so wrong, unjustified and ... perverse that I know a great many people are feeling very much for

Anna and hoping that you will succeed with an appeal'. He went on to say,

> That such a glaring miscarriage of justice has been allowed to occur is just another illustration of the failure by the courts to deal sympathetically and compassionately with women suffering from severe stress, and, in particular, post-natal depression. It is a sad reflection of . . . society that we should first convict somebody like her of murder and then subject them to a system of 'reform' which will only do her harm. Courts can and do get it wrong.

But what really surprised me, and perturbed me, coming as it did smack bang in the middle of my self-induced slide into Valium oblivion, was the proclamation at the end of this letter: 'It is only by a determined fight that justice in Anna's case will be done. A major campaign is under way and will not end until that justice is done.'

I was amazed that anyone wanted to save me – or thought for more than a moment that I was worth saving. I was secure, thank you very much, within my own prison and the walled one around me. I lived with dulled perception and darkened, distorted insight. All that was real to me was the passing of each day and the beginning of another one, and the support of my friends in the prison who also lived in the world of unreality by necessity. But it seemed that the campaign was taking effect. The local church leaders started to pray for me at every service, and the Catholics held novenas of prayer in monasteries and convents. They wrote continuously to the local papers, saying that they thought I should not stay in prison, but if I had to I should be treated with 'special care and sympathy'. Hmm.

Even stranger things were to come. A visitor brought with her a cutting from the agony column in the *Sun*. Headlined 'MY MAN'S TORMENT OVER HIS MURDER-JURY VERDICT', the letter read:

> My husband is desperately worried and upset because he sat on a jury which found someone guilty of

murder who was sentenced to life. The problem is that the jury reached their verdict because some of the members wanted to get home for the weekend. Now my husband can't get over it. You'd think that he was the judge who passed the sentence. The verdict of guilty to murder was brought by a 10–2 majority. But what's getting to him is that in the morning when the jury were sent out there were at least four people who believed it was manslaughter. Two changed their minds around 4.30p.m. Apparently they were worried they might have to spend the night in a hotel because an 8–4 majority was not acceptable to the judge. My husband is not very good with his words. He couldn't express himself well enough to get his point across. He feels that if he had been able to, the supposed murderer could have received desperately needed help rather than imprisonment. He feels that it was a mockery of British justice all because he couldn't convince those two people to stick to their original verdict rather than worry if they were going home for the weekend . . . .

My visitor had immediately telephoned the *Sun* to check if this was one of the jurors at my trial, and it appeared that indeed he was. It all seemed very, very peculiar to me that all these people were worrying themselves about someone as worthless as me. But it did not stop there. The Catholic sister who worked in Holloway brought me another cutting, this time from that establishment bastion, the *Daily Telegraph*. The piece was headed: 'The tragedy of Anna Reynolds'.

The Northampton evening paper had no doubts. When the trial was over, and it was time for adjectives, she was 'evil'. In twenty years of journalism, it is an adjective I have seen applied only to people like the Moors Murderers. What was more, much of the court evidence that the paper itself reported contradicted that.

I live just ten miles from Brackley, and can remember people's reactions. There was more pity than anything, a sense that something had gone terribly wrong. Last February, with the verdict, that had become incredulity. It is now outrage . . . .

Anna Reynolds' solicitor has said that he has never known so many members of the public get in touch to express concern over a jury verdict. In Brackley itself, and in the surrounding villages, a petition is circulating which looks like being signed by just about every adult resident.

The writer went on to describe the whole story with empathy and sensitivity. I was amazed. When I finished reading it I folded it up and put it away, near to tears. I did not know why I was crying, or for whom.

The next day, in the same paper, there was another article – an interview with the law student, Jonathan Marsh, and his mother, Judith. Next from the now obsessed media was a Radio 4 broadcast on *Woman's Hour*, with two guests unknown to me, Dr Katharina Dalton and Helena Kennedy, a barrister. Dr Dalton was, it emerged, a specialist on post-natal depression and pre-menstrual tension. Also on the panel were Judith Marsh and a girl with whom I had been at school.

They discussed the factor of pre-menstrual tension as it had arisen at the trial – Crown counsel had asked Dr O'Connor: 'Pre-menstrual tension has been mentioned in this case. Perhaps I can clear that out of the way. No such tension was involved in this young girl's case, was it?'

Dr O'Connor had replied: 'I do not think that pre-menstrual tension is a significant factor in this case.'

Crown counsel had suggested: 'It can then be discarded, can it?'

Dr Dalton was asked if it was reasonable for the defence in a murder trial to argue that post-natal depression could make a woman not fully responsible for her actions.

Yes, she replied, certainly it *was* possible for a woman to have a very severe psychosis complete with delusions, confusion, and loss of ability to think or to have any understanding of what she was doing. She could quite easily be so ill that she could commit murder. A large part of the programme was given over to discussion of the exact nature of pre-menstrual tension and post-natal depression, and then the panel turned to the issue of my actions and attitude in the witness box.

Helena Kennedy said that one of the things she felt about the case was that the jury seemed to have laid aside the 'very persuasive' medical evidence and saw before them a rather cool young woman, not crippled with emotional problems. When someone had suffered an emotional trauma, she went on, very often as a witness, they had to distance themselves from the events, which meant that in court they were quite often not quite what a jury expected. She likened the situation to that of the rape victim who doesn't appear to be ravaged by distress and emotion. Unfortunately no one had explained to the jury why, perhaps, Anna Reynolds wasn't coming over in the way they had anticipated.

Dr Dalton agreed and added: 'I would also feel that one of the characteristics of post-natal depression is these mood swings. She can appear calm in court, but that doesn't mean to say that the rest of the twenty-four hours she is calm.

Helena Kennedy finished by saying: 'We often forget that standing up in court just to give evidence is a very hard thing to do, and it sounds as though this young woman was actually subjected to cross-examination by various skilful prosecutors. It is so awful that there was this young woman standing up in court having to give her account, and yet she is measured and looked at in the cold light of day.'

I think Helena Kennedy was the one who came closest to seeing the turmoil that had lain behind the front at court. But that was all past, and I could not see why they wanted to rehash all this. I was frightened at the thought of more change. I wanted to stay in jail, to punish myself and be punished, and these people were trying to change that. It disturbed me.

I had difficulty in thinking about anything that was painful or raw, and that left very little. I had no resources left to deal with the soreness inside me, so I did not try, but instead let the drugs blank me out time and time again. The dosage got stronger, and the types changed. I was a tenacious addict, and carried with me a fierce and vague wish for oblivion. Nothing really worked anyway. I would wake early, after the initial knock-out, and burning with the need to hurt myself. I was inventive. I poured boiling water over me from the huge tea urn. I climbed into ice-cold or steaming hot baths until I could bear it no longer and climbed out again, tears of pain pouring down my face. I scrubbed the ovens and the long corridors until my hands were raw and red and my companions driven mad with helpless worry.

Sometimes, worn out with desperation and reflection and analysis, we laughed together – with relief that another day had passed, with friendship for each other, sometimes with a flicker of hope. The others would fall asleep quickly, stoned from their clandestine dope. But Mona and I would talk earnestly into the night – ideas were tossed over and discussed, advice given and exchanged. I felt a flow of sympathy, subtle, and unpatronizing; and uncompromising love, which I could not accept. I had never had a friend as selfless as Mona. She had a family to worry about, yet she gave a lot to me, undeserving creature that I was.

There came a time, the anniversary of Mum's death, when enough seemed to be enough – too much, even. I was determined, as the pain crept up on me slowly and achingly, that I would die this time. No more mistakes. I felt no great drama about this, but a need to be gone from the empty desolation of the incredibly long days when I cried so much, so silently, that my throat was always sore and my voice worn from sadness. I felt about a hundred years old.

It was easy. Every evening I was given, with foolish and unusually trusting abandon by the nurses, a large dose of chloral hydrate, the old-fashioned sleeping draught. Everyone on the wing craved it, but I was the lucky one for whom it was prescribed. At first it sent me high enough to hit the ceiling, but after a period of wariness I settled down to a warm and loving relationship with it and waited each evening for the medicine cabinet to come round. It would wend its creaky and maddeningly slow way around the prison until it reached our door and ground to a halt. It seemed to come round later and later each evening, until I was clamouring at the hatch and wanting to ring the emergency bell to ask where the much-needed medical supplies were. I was persuaded that this would not be a good idea.

The nurse was supposed to watch you to check that you had swallowed it all. She did not. I smiled and nodded before I spat the drug into the empty cup I held. For weeks and months I saved it up, quite unknown to the officers. Suddenly I became aware that if our dorm were to be searched my little hoard would be discovered. I was devious in my hour of need. I needed as much of the stuff as possible to ensure that the job was done properly this time. I emptied it all from the cup into an old moisturizer bottle. After a while Mona noticed and asked if she could have a drop to help her sleep. I agreed, of course.

Come the night I decided to make my last, I emptied the stuff into a cup and drank it down with a drop of precious, rare orange squash. Nothing happened for a while, then sleep came, slowly and unhappily. I stayed asleep for at least a day, woken at intervals to crawl to the kitchen to refuse meals and crawl back again. When at last I woke, confused and miserable, with an awful headache and a dry mouth, Mona told me that she had guessed what I was up to and had emptied a lot of the chloral out and replaced it with water, leaving enough to dope me but not kill me. God! It seemed I was dogged by salvationists.

Soon after this little episode I was forced to see a psychiatrist. I had been blissfully unaware of the fact that, now I was a life-sentenced prisoner, I would have to be continually assessed by shrinks to see how the sentence had affected me, how I felt at different points about the offence, how stable I was and so on. I had presumed that after the sentencing I would be left alone to wallow and decay in my own time, and that I would not have to see any more of the mind-probers I dreaded so much. I resented their intrusion, the way they picked their path indelicately through the minefield of my emotions and then walked away sharply and precisely after the time was up, leaving me to cope with what they had laid bare and raw.

I was unusual still in that I could not readily talk about the deepest cuts and almost never on demand, except when it was wrenched out of me by some forceful shrink determined to have something to write to prove he had indeed seen me. And this one they had chosen was the pits. He was the same one who had delivered the report at the trial saying that I was a matter for a jury, not a psychiatrist. Hmm. Things change.... I sat and said nothing, waiting politely for him to speak and tell me what he required of me. He too sat silent. The minutes ticked by and I grew hot and worried, feeling sweat in my palms. Eventually I asked him what I was supposed to say. In reply he asked what made me think I was supposed to say anything in particular. I said that I thought somebody ought to or we would be there all day. He raised his eyebrows as if to say, 'Are you in a hurry? Do you have somewhere else to go?' I thought about the trial, when he had appeared in his 'uniform' of long dark leather coat with tinted glasses and leather boots, looking for all the world like a shady detective from the films. The real ones wear blue nylon Home Office trousers and cheap tweed jackets that do not fit properly over their straining pot bellies.

The session ended in exactly one hour, after this man had told me in a slow monotone about his travel phobias and sat and rolled the sleep he had picked out of the corner of his eyes. He looked continually and pointedly at his watch and rolled his eyes to Heaven, perhaps in hope of divine deliverance. I knew with utter conviction that I did not and had never needed psychiatry. Apart from anything else, I found it too patronizing to accept the unequal balance of me on the inferior side of the desk, the mad patient, waiting breathless for pearls of wisdom to fall from the doctor's mouth as he sat behind the desk, pen in hand or even tape recorder going. I thought of them as hit-and-miss artists who used their arrogance as a means to cover lack of knowledge. But I knew of no alternative therapy. I had heard of analysis, of psychotherapy, but since I was told by the psychiatrists that they could practise these upon me if I wished I saw no point in any of them.

I knew, though, after all that had happened, that I was not all right. I wanted the Valium and the sleeping drugs and the convenient haze of not knowing or caring to envelop me completely. I seemed to be trapped by my own volition in a downward spiral of self-hatred, guilt and despair. Life was not worth living, but death didn't seem to be too easy to come by, either. How did that Russian quotation go? 'Life is not so good, but then death is not so pleasant either . . . . '

And then, somehow, like a shining, fresh, hopeful breath of life came Carol Gotlieb. She was a probation officer who worked in the prison, and she came on a crusade to save those whom she recognized as being near enough the edge to fall right over. A trained counsellor, she took me to her cheery, card-filled little office and sat me down with a cup of real coffee, such a luxury, and heard me introduce myself as someone who had just received a life sentence and was supposed to be psychopathic and have a personality disorder. She was a little taken aback by this abrupt, mechanical introduction from someone who had, she said afterwards, 'dead eyes and a lifeless voice'. But she did not show her surprise or appear put off. I talked and talked and talked, a ceaseless and probably meaningless flow of words which were purely to fill the gap that might have allowed Carol to ask any painful questions.

Suddenly she just said firmly: 'Stop.' I did, out of surprise. I had never been told to stop talking. Before the end of my first session with her she had decided that I had to stop talking and start allowing myself to feel once again, instead of strangling the emotions with words. I had never thought of it quite as bluntly as that, never faced my fear. She explained to me exactly what counselling was, how it was based upon equality between the client (never patient) and the counsellor, an equal contract being exchanged in which each person decided what they wanted to work on, work through, change or discover in themselves. I knew that the time had come to take a massively deep breath and go forward into reality again before it was too late. I trusted her straightaway – her honesty and her generosity in giving as much during the counselling to heal me as she got back. After the first session I felt slightly scared, but freer, as if I had blindly sought the key to my own secrets and had started the unlocking.

Carol warned me that it would be the most painful time of all, the laying out of my life and deciding what I had to let go from the past and what I must keep. We used all sorts of techniques, games, to winkle these ghosts out of me, and into the recesses of my memory and soul we delved together, on an expedition to find the truth. And we came near enough to that for me to get through the days with less and less aid from Valium and the like. I did not stop completely, but the habit was now controllable.

One day our short and much-valued session was interrupted by a stern-faced officer who told me I was wanted on the wing. The mood was broken harshly and I made a face at Carol, who winked and ushered me out of the office with a pat on the shoulder. Back on the wing I stood outside the office wondering what I had done, my reaction to a summons from authority being an automatic one from childhood. I soon found out. I had done nothing this time, but my allocation had come through. This was the placement I would go to – in more colloquial language the prison where I would spend the biggest chunk of my sentence. I had been told by the nasty Gestapo-dressed doctor that I would stay at Holloway for at least eighteen months to face therapy. This therapy had so far consisted of two sessions one month apart. The officer looked at me and told me that I was to go to H Wing Durham on the next escort.

I started crying before I had even left the office, to my great shame and the male officer's discomfort. I was crying with fear. H Wing was for lifers, what was known as a Category A prison, but I had been told I would not go there. I was eighteen and too young for there, they said. The Catholic sister intervened, the prison governor listened to her and the allocation was put off. I was reprieved – for now. I felt that time was running out, though.

The day came, inevitably, when the allocation could not

be stopped. I was told to pack up my things and be ready the next morning. I wrote to everyone, telling them where I was going. Ironically, that day a letter had arrived from Roy enclosing a copy of a legal document from the Appeal Court. It did not immediately make sense to me, so I took it to the wing officer and we phoned Roy to check. It said that 'the Honourable Mr Justice Rose ... grants legal aid to the appellant for the following purpose: the preparation and presentation of an appeal against conviction, the Single Judge having granted Leave to Appeal.'

This was actually quite a big step. The stages of an appeal were that one judge had to grant leave to appeal before the case could be heard. It was extremely rare for the single judge to do this. I was surprised, and now it seemed even sillier for me to go so far north when in all likelihood I would have to be down south for legal visits, court appearances and so on. But I could do nothing about the course of events.

The journey to Durham took seven tedious hours in a cramped van with barred windows. Eventually we turned into a small town and ascended a hill. It was beginning to get dark. At the summit I could see a huge, turreted building of dark grey stone.

'That's it,' said one of the Holloway screws. 'That's H Wing. The Jail on the Hill, they call it. That's your new home.'

Chapter Nine

In 1961 one wing of Durham prison was used for a special security and punishment block for male escapees. In 1965 it was converted for the arrival of the Great Train Robbers and the Kray twins. Then named E Wing, it was seldom out of the headlines in the 1960s due to hunger strikes, protests and a major riot. Two reports about the wing came to the same conclusion. Earl Mountbatten's report, *The Regime for Long Term Prisoners in Conditions of Maximum Security*, was of the opinion that 'the conditions ... are such that no country with a record of civilized behaviour ought to tolerate any longer than is absolutely necessary as a stop-gap measure.'

The Radzinowicz Report confirmed this but was slightly less emotive in its comments: 'No one regards the containment of prisoners in such small, confined units as anything other than a temporary and most undesirable expedient. The physical limitations of the buildings preclude any major improvement in the conditions.'

Mainly as a result of these reports E Wing was closed, and by 1971 all the prisoners had been dispersed elsewhere within the prison system. Then £100,000 was spent on upgrading security to prevent escapes such as those of Walter Probyn and John McVicar ever happening again. In due course the wing was reopened as H Wing, with spaces for thirty-eight top security women prisoners. That was in 1974, when there was only one Category A woman prisoner in the country. Women serving short sentences at a nearby remand centre were sent to H Wing to make the numbers up and justify the wing being kept open.

In 1984 the report of the Chief Inspector of Prisons stated that it

> is not possible to offer a change of environment either for the individual prisoner's good or to help staff deal with a group of violent inmates. Thus, the four Category A prisoners have been in H Wing for three years or more. We think this restriction operates against the interests of the prisoners and of staff and we formally recommend the Prison Department should provide a second outlet for female Category A prisoners.

There are several prisons in England where long-term and Category A prisoners can be placed – as long as they are male: Frankland, Gartree, Wormwood Scrubs, Parkhurst, Albany on the Isle of Wight, and Leicester, among others. So at least a male prisoner with a life sentence or a Category A status can be expected to be moved fairly often and to be in the region where his family and friends live.

In the September 1989 issue of *Briefings*, the newsletter for the prison service, the Director-General lays down these facts about life-sentence prisoners and their treatment and accommodation:

> A life sentence is indeterminate . . . two factors govern release: the period required for punishment, and an assessment of the risk to the community. For those convicted of very grave crimes the first review date is after seventeen years. Young offenders (life sentence) go direct to a training institution. Women go to Durham or to Bullwood Hall.

A young offender is someone under twenty-one years of age. I was eighteen when I went to H Wing.

Women in Prison, a campaigning group, wrote to the Home Office about H Wing:

We have spoken to several women who have served sentences in Durham about the issue of visits – one woman spoke of not seeing her four children for a year. The DHSS would not pay for them and an adult to travel so far, saying that the journey with an overnight stay would be too expensive. This is not an isolated case; she and others spoke of the immense strain for them and their children of accumulated visits only once or twice a year.

This sentiment was borne out by the inspectorate report on H Wing. The Chief Inspector admitted that the 'uniqueness' of Durham presented difficulties; 'It is not geographically convenient for a national resource; 50 per cent of inmates in H Wing are from the south and therefore contact with children, relatives and friends is difficult to maintain.'

I, of course, was ignorant of the history of H Wing. All I knew, with a sigh of relief, was that it was a real prison. It was jail, grim and grey, hopeless and soul-weary. It fulfilled all my expectations of awfulness and all my visions of a place designed specifically for punishment.

It was a huge building, the women's wing surrounded by the male prison, a messy, sprawling remand and short-term sentence place. The outside, the receptions area, was pale stone, new and sleek, a deception to the eye. Inside the main gates, one passed through two more sets of gates into an open space that led to an ancient building of dark, dirty grey stone. Myriad tiny windows, criss-crossed with bars so that the interiors were completely invisible. Pigeon shit everywhere. Shouting, the sounds of abuse, of sickness, the smell of rotten food. As we drew up to the fence, lit with plentiful security cameras, I saw pails of stinking, overflowing slops. Inside the fence, I was not heartened by the maze of gates with security locks that we still had to pass through. Silently the screws waited at each gate until the surveillance camera had sussed us out and opened the gate automatically. Naturally a tidy person, I pulled one to behind me.

'Don't you dare touch that gate! It's a breach of security!' barked the officer.

A voice spoke from the intercom at the third gate. 'What's going on?'

'Inmate touched gate no. 3,' said the officer, glaring at me.

I did not dare to ask why it was a breach of security. I knew with an immediate and awful certainty that the answer would not be sensible. The officer pushed me inside the final gate and, blinking and scrunching up my eyes, I was at last inside the wing.

The first thing was the light. Huge pools of glaring, harsh fluorescent light, the dull pneumatic glare assaulting my tired eyes. The wing itself was small for thirty-eight women and an inordinate number of staff. It went up and up, landing after landing, perimeters of cell doors with the open centre covered by wire netting to prevent any would-be suicide leaps. Bars, the dim gleam of metal upon metal, tarnished surfaces well oiled for ease of locking. Little noise, surprisingly, after the brash chaos of Holloway, the milling round of women, of laughter, sobbing, chatter, fights. The predominant colour was grey. The grey of metal buckets, doors, bars and locks. And keys, of course.

That first evening on the wing passed in a blur of trying to accustom myself to its newness and strangeness. The next day, to my pleasure, another woman came from a remand prison. The novelty of my being a new face dissipated in the wake of a second newcomer. Sarah was vastly similar to me in her guilt and acknowledgement of her need for flagellation. She hated the wing as soon as she arrived and we became friends, pacifying each other in that harsh place by constantly reminding ourselves that it was What We Needed.

Disgust took the place of other emotions when we discovered that there were no toilets in the cells and we had to 'slop out' between lock-up at 7p.m. and unlock in the morning. Underneath the bed reposed a small white plastic pot, not so clean either, for use during the night or even the day if we were not unlocked because of the frequent staff shortage. Pots were passed on from one inmate to another. At first we made a pact not to use them for fear of losing our last vestiges of self-respect and dignity, but soon bladder pain overcame the loathing and we had to line up with everyone else who had gone through the same dilemma on entering the wing and empty the things into a huge sluice next to the washbasins and communal toilets. Later in the morning – not very much later, in fact just after breakfast – my job would be to clean these sluices thoroughly. We had no rubber gloves, disinfectant or mops. We just had cloths which we then used to clean the sink, and a scouring pad which was also used generally. Leaning over the loo the first time, throwing up at the stench, I pondered the irony of being so literally in the shit where I felt I belonged. ('The purpose of the treatment and training of convicted prisoners should be to encourage them to lead a good and useful life on release.' Prison Rule No. 1.)

One day, these dreaded sluices, the bane of my life, burst their banks. Enough was enough, they cried, and lifting up their lids they died. First thing in the morning thirty-eight women had emptied their potties down them, probably complete with used sanitary towels, tampons and so on. Where else would they put them, heavy with blood, in the middle of the night? The main sluice, the one on the ground floor, suddenly overflowed violently. At the time we were all queuing for breakfast, and some women already eating theirs. The breakfast area was next to the sluice. We were instructed to fetch brooms and buckets and cloths and to set our hands to the stinking floor. As before, we had no mops, no rubber gloves, no disinfectant. We pushed old cloths around on the end of brooms, then picked the cloths up and wrung them out into a bucket. After the worst had been removed we were told that we could carry on with our breakfast. No, thank you. No one was that eager to get food poisoning.

After quite a few episodes like this, and with the onslaught of winter when the pipes would freeze up, one of the women decided it was time to make a stand. One morning, as so often before, the sluices overflowed. Heads poked out of office doors. The usual shouts of remonstration came. Nobody moved. None of us intended clearing up again a mess that was a product of the Victorian plumbing system. The shouts got louder and angrier and threats of the punishment block were made. Direct orders were issued. The leader of the revolt eyed the weaker women with ferocity. Nobody moved. They dared not. Sarah and I wanted to giggle – it was such a battle of wills. Eventually tempers got higher and higher and the threats got more threatening. Some of the women had visits from their children that day and did not want to forego them, so they trailed down guiltily to help clear up. Satisfied, the staff retreated into the safety of their offices. Everyone else was locked in as a punishment for refusing to clear up their own shit twice in one morning.

I don't think, on reflection, that any of us knew how to cope with life on the wing. It was an unnatural way to live. We had weekly cell and body searches, when the cell and all your belongings were turned upside down to see if you had any drugs hidden there, brought in by the visitors you didn't have because they lived in Plymouth or somewhere equally remote. There was a spyhole in the door, so that you could be watched silently even when you were reluctantly peeing on the nasty pot; the light switch was outside so that you could not control even that much of your life. You could not see out of the window unless you stood on the bed on tiptoe, and even then all you could see was the men's prison. In winter, it was freezing. Even in summer we wore three layers of clothes and gloves in bed. We scrubbed the wing day after day, polishing the floor and carrying huge boxes of laundry around. We cleaned as best we could with no materials, but then a poor workman always blames her tools, they would have said.

And sometimes, albeit rarely and with the edge of desperation, we laughed. Once, in H Wing, something happened. Sarah saw a leaf fall from the top floor and we wondered how on earth it had penetrated the security of the building. 'How will it get out again, that's the thing,' she said. We giggled at this. Another friend walked past. 'That's no leaf,' she said. Another of her toyshop tricks, I thought. I went to retrieve it and hand it back to her to play her joke elsewhere. An officer came towards it and screamed: 'It's not a joke one! God. How stupid do you think I am?' Diplomatically I did not reply to this but examined it. Sure enough, it was a real live mouse, or rather a real dead one, having hara-kiried its way from the fourth floor, neatly missing all three lots of netting. So much for the suicide wire.

Apart from this mindless, pointless bloody cleaning, there was nothing else to do except think, and watch, and absorb. Oh, you could cook, by the way, there was a kitchen for the women to use at evenings and weekends, provided after some of the inmates had campaigned for it. You could make cakes, meals, etc, – that is if you could afford to buy the ingredients out of your £3 weekly wage. But basically, that was tip-of-the-iceberg stuff. Thirty-eight women together on a little wing resulted in a lot of petty tension and quite a lot of real friction. Fights occurred as the result of all the bottling up of both mind and body that was a necessity unless you wanted to spend all your time on the block. There was one time when, due to staff shortages, we were locked in from Friday afternoon after work until Monday morning work; because, whatever else happens, the wing must be cleaned. Several times. Then some male officers in big dirty wet boots can come in and walk all over the nice clean shiny floor, and then – well, that's the afternoon's work lined up for you. Isn't that neat?

It was December that weekend when we were locked in, and the heating wasn't working. We sat in our respective cells freezing to death. I had a period, and as usual it was very heavy. We were only allowed one sanitary towel or two tampons at a time in case we tried to eat them or something. I dripped blood everywhere. The pot was full of blood, clots and all. The sheets were two-day soiled with blood, because sheet change was once a week. One sheet once a week.

Sometimes there was a peculiar solidarity between us on the wing, as in the sluice-fight. Then it dissolved under pressure. There had been other issues on the wing, hunger strikes and the like, when the women had also started out as a solid force and been worn down by the staff. The wing itself wore you down – no one could stand it for long without a compromise or two. The building itself seemed to drain the life from your body: tall and huge and dark, even in the harshness of that fluorescence. There was a perpetual coldness in the stone walls that made your bones ache with damp. Summer or winter it was indifferent to the passing of the seasons, as were the occupants, who could neither see nor feel the heat or sun-rays while they were within its walls. My eyesight grew steadily worse and I could not face daylight in the daily half-hour exercise in the tiny yard, overlooked by the male prisoners shouting abuse. Migraines and headaches were so common an occurrence among the women that some were on a regular daily dose of painkiller.

I came to see why the women who had been on H Wing for quite a while (one woman had been there for fourteen years, another for seven, and several for over four years) had a shared look of dullness, as if their minds were closed to anything but the survival of each day. They looked as though they were moving in a drugged dream, their faces deadened, their bodies automatically slackened in response to their lifestyle, their movements tailored to commands given and obeyed.

With the aim of putting off that mental stagnation for as long as possible I went to the prison library. There I found a mass of self-help books – *How To Cope with Depression, How to Cope with Tranquillizer Withdrawal, How to Come to Terms with Loss* – but none called *How to Cope with H Wing*. I found Walter Probyn's autobiography *Angel Face*, in which I read these words from a Home Office White Paper: 'The prisoner's contacts with the outside world are the bridge over which he can pass back into decent society, and under no circumstances must these contacts be undermined. By restriction and distance you are virtually suppressing the contacts you publicly declare are vital rehabilitative factors.' I also found Jean Harris's tale of life in a US maximum security jail, *Stranger in Two Worlds*, in which she wrote: 'Prison discipline has little to do with wrongdoing. It has a great deal to do with how people feel about you, or how fearful the staff are of the people who complain about you.' She added, with great directness, that the 'trauma of waking to a daily nightmare in which people whose judgement you have little respect for control you totally is nightmare alley'.

I went away armed with books and read with a thirst I had not experienced for a long time. Eagerly I scanned the Stan Cohen/Laurie Taylor collaboration *Psychological Survival*. They make the point that the conditions in a maximum-security jail are different from any other kind of imprisonment, and produce in the prisoner

> a desperate and intolerable strain. There is no escape from it. The public are paying the sum of £256 [now nearer £700 at 1989 estimates for maximum-security conditions] to keep prisoners in such destructive conditions that are calculated to turn its victims into the same kind of homicidal maniac that US prisons produce. They are paying that sum to have inflicted upon them at a future date a new breed of criminal who will be as brutal, ruthless and destructive against society as it has been against him.

But while all this inner reflection was burning inside me, down south things were happening. The wheels of the appeal machine were beginning to turn and churn, bringing nearer the date which I had firmly put out of my mind. The media were still interested. *Bella* magazine featured the case. Esther Rantzen and *Rough Justice* were interested in filming around it. It seemed the world wanted me to be other than where I was. The staff in H Wing, who I thought without much interest to be hang-em-and-flog-em types, were very much wanting the appeal to be a success. Everyone seemed to think it would be settled before the year was over.

More psychiatry came my way, all in aid of the appeal. A doctor from Newcastle came to examine my mind. He thought it was highly likely that 'it was a fine line between your mother and the baby, and that had you kept the baby, I do not hesitate to predict that the baby would have been killed, with you in the state you were then'.

At that time Roy wrote to tell me that he wanted me to come to Holloway to see Dr Katharina Dalton, the pre-menstrual syndrome expert who had been on the radio. He had applied to the Home Office and I would be transferred soon. So down to Holloway I went in the last days of August 1987. I saw Dr Dalton, who instructed me to keep menstrual records and told me that I would be given a blood test to determine whether or not I had PMS. I was a bit shaken and stirred by all this action, which seemed very abrupt and decided to me. When had I ever said that I had PMS, anyway? All my 'supporters' were now pinning their hopes firmly on the PMS angle, but I was afraid that it would be one more wind-up.

Back in Holloway I became a nervous wreck. I had moved around with ease in H Wing, so small that you knew everyone and had to explain nothing. Here there were unfamiliar faces and they frightened me. They were curious. I was nineteen and I was from the notorious H Wing. What had I done to go there? What was it like there? I could not face this barrage of questions, so I did not come out of the cell except to refuse meals; on my return I would sink back into a stupor and bite my nails. I felt unprotected by the comparative laxness of the routine at Holloway after H Wing's strictness. Here I had to think for myself and make occasional decisions. Also I could have visits here, which I did not really want: I had nothing to say to anyone.

After three weeks, the Powers That Be moved me back to H Wing. I was thankful to be back where I would not find any challenges except that of staying alive and, more difficult, lively. The bare bleakness of the wing soothed me, its austerity a balm to my guilt.

Soon I was taken up to the nursing office for my blood test. The nurse tried. It could not be said that she did not. The veins in both arms were redundant. She tried them twice each. No luck. My wrists were jabbed. Nothing there either. The thought crossed my mind that, given each monthly torrent, it was possible I had none to spare for a blood test. Eventually the nurse got cross, fetched a really huge needle and jabbed it in my left arm. Blood spurted all over me, the nurse and her snow-white uniform – in fact everywhere but the syringe. I had large, alarming bruises the next day where she had tried to insert the needle, but she no sample had.

Later that week, the nurse managed to get her blood sample and told me it was winging its way to London to be treated and analysed. I cared little – even less because I had just been told in a hasty letter from Roy that the adoption hearing was on 18 December. It was the end of November by the time I was notified, and he apologized. I had wavered about signing the final papers for two reasons. I was aware that by putting up a fight I might be able to hold off the hearing until after the appeal, which the adopters' solicitors had agreed to some time back; and I thought that, even if I lost, Alex might one day know that I had tried as hard as I could with both hands tied behind my back.

First of all I had the little problem of getting permission to go to the hearing. I didn't have much time, and it was always a laborious business getting anything from the Home Office. After petitioning again and again, and writing and plaguing the Wing Governor and the principal officer, I was told that I could attend. I was to go the night before and then stay in Holloway for a few days before returning to Durham.

Once again I was off. I seemed to spend more time in transit than justified ever sending me up here in the first place. Now I had to face the worst of all, the last part of the saga of my past. So south I headed once again.

Chapter Ten

The court, it seemed, had refused to hold off any longer on the question of waiting for the appeal hearing before going ahead with the one about Alex's adoption. It seemed silly to me that they wanted to get things tied up hurriedly now before the slim chance of my being free came to pass.

When the day came I had slept little the night before. I dressed smartly, in some vain attempt to try to impress the judge that I was a sensible and sane person. The hearing was in St Albans. We arrived early, and I looked around for Roy. Instead I saw his clerk hurrying towards me; he was extremely cheerful, but gave no indication of familiarity with the matter to go before the court.

That morning passed before my eyes with painful clarity. The events that were chewed over were the same ones as always. I was so used to court rooms now that they did not really intimidate me any longer.

The process did not take very long. The plain-clothed officers with me looked away and seemed to have a rough kind of sympathy. But the hearing dealt me blows that I felt must surely be mortal ones. I was not expecting such a cruel and swift condemnation of my character. The social worker who was speaking on behalf of the people they called the 'parents' – here I glared, hateful, at the social worker collective – was nervous, and inadvertently gave away the name and address of the adopters, a fatal mistake. The court officials obviously thought that at the slightest opportunity I would go round to the house and – do what? They seemed to have forgotten for a split second the confinement I was in. They never forgot it at any other time. My hopelessly ineffective barrister, scarcely out of pupilage, unfamiliar with my story and with the case in hand, did not press for a delayed hearing but tried to give a defence for the adoption. I was furious and helpless. I had no recourse to my own defence without looking irresponsible and unstable.

When the time came for the Guardian Ad Litem to speak her piece, the court was told fretfully, with reproving glances cast in my direction, that the mother of the child was 'withholding her agreement unreasonably'. The legal position in the House of Lords ruling is that the courts have to place the greatest emphasis on what is best for the child rather than what is best for the parent. The problem here was obvious: although the sections about neglect of or harm to the child, or lack of love and care, did not apply, the one that asked 'Is there a serious defect in the mental condition, stability of character and temperament or the mode of living in the parent which could be harmful to the child?' did. So did the one that followed: 'Is there a reasonable prospect of the parent being able to provide a home for the child?'

I was seen as 'the mother who on her own admission is not in a position to so provide but who withholds her agreement to adoption because to give it would break the natural bond and give the impression that she had abandoned her child unreasonably'. There was no ruling laid down on the procedure for parents who were awaiting appeal decisions. I could make no assurances in that direction – all I wanted and expected was a postponement. Again the scorching glances. 'It is felt that this has dragged on long enough. The parents' (there it is again, that legally incorrect and oh so painful word. What right had they to that description? They could not produce a child, and that was why they wanted mine.) 'have suffered too long the indecision. The mother has suffered from nervous problems and is taking Valium, and the father is now having problems at work.'

I was now caught in an intolerable dilemma. I was to go on the witness stand and face the judge, who was female but as hard and uncompromisingly disdainful of me as a man might be – and was in another trap. If my attitude and demeanour were seen to be unstable no one would think me fit to be a mother, but if I were seen to be perfectly fine then my conviction would be seen as evidence of evil, not of madness. Once again I could not win and once again, it seemed, I was on trial. I was weary with being tried over and over again and found wanting in so many people's eyes.

On that day I was fighting for the right to be a mother to the child I had bled and wept over. I knew that I had lost before it started. The social worker for the 'other side' smiled helplessly at me. I glared at her through a mist of tears that I dared not let slip. Soon afterwards I received a letter from her asking if I would like to see her; only to tell you what I think of you, I thought grimly. She continued that she hoped by now I had recovered from my 'sad experience' (that was three days later – is that the going rate for recovery of a lost child?) and that she was aware that I had avoided 'eye contact' with her.

After the hearing I sat numbly on the bench – another hard wooden bench to add to my collection – while the surprisingly tactful screws tiptoed out of the vicinity. There I sat, flanked by the equally useless clerk and barrister. They were flustered by the speed and unexpected decision and were speechless. For the first time the tears came, and I made no effort to stop them . . . I hadn't the strength. The barristers, in an insane attempt to cheer me up, started telling me some of the behind-the-scenes events that had apparently taken place at the trial. Nothing could possibly be any worse now. There was almost a dull satisfaction as my inner voice, the conscience substitute, told me: 'There! It's all for the good of the Catholic soul.'

We lingered a while in the now silent court room for me to get myself together. Back in the car we sat squeezed up together, from necessity rather than choice: the officers were both big women and it was a relatively small car. We did not dare to look at each other, so close were we. To draw an extra-deep breath one had to turn sideways as diplomatically as possible. I stared down at my hands and did not allow myself to think about the events of the day.

That would come later when I was back in Holloway. I desperately wanted to get back to the relative peace of a locked cell and let loose inside me the devils of pain who were even now howling and clamouring for release. I dreaded the long, long wait in the receptions area that was surely inevitable.

Later, dragging myself up to the hatch on the door in receptions, I recognized an officer who had befriended me on one of the wings. She came over to me, exclaiming in disbelief at my white face and dull eyes, telling me that I was a different girl from the one who had gone to Durham only a while back. Was it only a while back? It seemed an awesome eternity to me.

Up on the wing at last I slunk over to the bed, utterly exhausted, and sat in a stupor of half-belief. It had come to this, then, finally: that there was nothing left to hold on for. I wrote in my diary:

> Now at last I don't have any reasons left to live, let alone to care... today is a day on which I would gladly die. I am too afraid to sleep, because of the nightmares. Not that sleep would come easily to me now anyway. I cannot keep these wolves of pain at bay any longer. Oh God... how can I bear it? I don't want to see anyone. No one at all.

In the cell I had found myself, to my ungrateful dismay, surrounded by flowers from well-intentioned but misguided campaigners. A fresh flood of sobs racked me. I loved flowers, but on that day it seemed a cruel tribute to the court's decision. I sat on the floor and dripped on to the bunches of winter colour.

That night I did not sleep; I did not expect to. What peace would there be for me except nightmares and an awakening to more tears? I lay flat on the hard metal bed and schooled my mind not to think about it any more. I went back deliberately into the dream-world of the past, where the landscape was full of white-painted cottages, smoking chimneys and rosy-cheeked children. I realized how this was going to affect my daily reaction to everything. I would have to be careful when opening the pages of a magazine – not that we often saw such things – and be wary of the pictures of babies. Just as when I had been very pregnant, the pictures and adverts seemed to contain nothing but nappies and fat gurgling babes, happy, contented mothers, dungarees and heartbreakingly tiny shoes for equally tiny feet. These images haunted me daily and at night crept into my dreams when I slept, which was less and less.

It was now nearing Christmas and I wanted to be shipped back to the relentless northern chill of Durham. I knew with a dullness born mostly from the lethargy of true depression that I was not 'normal' any more. I wanted to go back to H Wing for all the wrong reasons. I wanted the silence that typifies the wing. I wanted the coldness that would match my emotions. I craved the loneliness of soul that I could have there. I craved the routine, strict and harsh as any POW camp, which released me from the torture of decisions and responsibilities. I craved the knowledge that back there, in the worst of conditions, I was where I belonged, where 'bad' people truly were.

Christmas at Holloway went on without any contribution from me, of course – others could celebrate, with that dreadful false heartiness that accompanies the festive season inside jail. Paper hats were handed out grimly, the bare walls were strung with paper chains and old, bald tinsel. Old records of carols were put on the record player and creaked round raspily. On the day itself, small, tight potatoes and some rather manky-looking chicken breast, the Bernard Matthews type, lay on the plates, congealing. I felt sick and refused. Black looks were cast at me from officers and inmates alike. I was being seen as a spoilsport, a misery. Sod them, I thought grimly.

I cried on Christmas night, on that night and every night following. Not a wet onslaught of petulance, but huge, dry, racking sobs that rent me and left me tired and sore-eyed. The prison staff worried at my constant refusal of food. I hardly noticed the passing of time, so caught up was I with the hugeness of this overwhelming and devastating last grief. This, then, was the midnight of Keats' despair, this wish to

> *... fade far away, dissolve and quite forget*
> *... the weariness, the fever and the fret*
> *Where but to think is to be full of sorrow*
> *And leaden-eyed despairs.*
> *... I cannot see what flowers are at my feet*
> *Nor what soft incense hangs upon the boughs.*
> *Darkling I listen; and for many a time*
> *I have been half in love with easeful Death.*

How well I knew this, how keenly it bit into me and reinforced my realization that

> *Now more than ever seems it rich to die*
> *To cease upon the midnight with no pain.*

This I was not ready for, but it had reached me anyway, regardless, and I was helpless to stench the flow of poison that circulated within me.

Chapter Eleven

Things got worse, and it seemed to last forever. The despair reached new depths and nothing could drag me up. I did not want to be lifted out of it – there was nothing to replace it. I spoke little, through almost clenched teeth. Most of the time I was almost unconscious with misery. When I was not, a primal scream raged within me and shook my frame.

They delayed taking me back to H Wing, for some untold reason. But it didn't matter – the feeling would tear me apart with its wild teeth wherever I was. One day they came into my room and told me I had to go and scrub a corridor. Until then I had spent all day sitting by the window staring out into the grounds of the prison, jumping nervously when my silence was disturbed by the door opening for breakfast, lunch or dinner to be announced. I would then have to walk to the dining room to refuse food – this had to be done to keep a check on who was eating and who was not. When they came to me to tell me that I must scrub the floor I laughed. It seemed ridiculous that I should have to do anything so unproductive as scrub a floor over which a thousand people would walk during that day and dirty it all over again.

I was not then quite ready to dare to flout the system and disobey rules. One of my biggest fears had always been the horrors of the block – the punishment cells – and how I would survive if I had to go down there. So I rose and walked unsteadily to the corridor. I had not eaten for a week or two and hardly drunk anything either. Now I was feeling the effects. I scrubbed half-heartedly. The officer with us beamed at me.

'That's right, luv,' she said. 'Nice to see you out of your room. Cheered up now, have you? Mustn't let it get you down. Every cloud has a silver lining.'

Christ, I thought, more clichés. I smiled a frozen smile and felt those rarely used facial muscles ache.

After what seemed an eternity of endless days, weeks like this, I went back to H Wing. I can't remember if I had any visitors. I registered nothing except the pit of despair into which I had sunk.

Back in Durham I was welcomed anxiously by Sarah and the other women who had both written letters to me while I was in Holloway. Sarah's had read: 'Don't worry love. Just you come back to us and we will make it all all right . . . .' I fell into Sarah's arms and sobbed as I had done silently all the way back up the motorway. She prepared coffee from her precious store and cakes from the batch she had made to welcome me back. 'You look as though you haven't eaten,' she said.

'I haven't,' I replied. I ate her cakes, though.

When in H Wing, scrub as the H Wingers scrub. That was the rule, and dully I obeyed it. To begin with it was almost a relief to have a routine that I had no choice but to obey. The work was hard, and the wing was cold with a chill born of the ancient walls and the curious lack of noise or healthy emotion. We were worker ants going about our dutiful designated business.

I functioned OK, but function was all it was. I breathed, I moved, I did as I was instructed – but only just. I was overcome by a huge and sweeping lethargy which woke me up exhausted and lasted all day, stopped me from the respite of sleep and made the days even more long and intolerable than usual. The work became far too much for me; I felt weak and dizzy with the effort of holding all my pain in day after day after day. Sweeping and scrubbing the already spotless landings, I ached with barely disguised anguish. Officers asked me what was the matter. I merely shook my head. I could not always trust myself to speak these days.

One day an officer walked over the wet, freshly scrubbed surface that I had laboured over all that morning. It was a purposeful action, because there was an alternate route that most of them used to avoid this happening. I looked up from my kneeling position and saw her standing there, insolent.

'This floor's dirty, Anna. You'll just have to do it all again, won't you? . . . And *before* dinner, by the way.'

I sat back on my heels and looked up at her for a long time before speaking. 'It's your fault.'

'I beg your pardon? Did I hear right?'

I looked around. There was a fire bucket near me, full of icy water. I looked up again tiredly. Where would it get me? I knew that these officers were particularly vicious when they were crossed and I was barely coping on the wing as it was, without being put into seclusion for emptying the bucket over her head. Head down, I scrubbed away. I figured that if I concentrated solely on the floor and thought of nothing else, I would get through the rest of the day. I never dared think about how I would survive the morrow. That was far too ambitious a prospect.

I had been given sleeping medicine since being back on the wing. Its only effect was to make me feel a bit woozy for ten minutes or so, like being nicely drunk, but then it wore off abruptly, leaving me feeling anti-climactic. Night after night I lay dry-eyed and relentlessly awake. The mornings found me shattered and uncommunicative. I knew that I was going headlong towards some sort of explosion, and I had no idea how to stop it or even if I wanted to. I felt hopelessly out of control and too wearily uncaring to try to halt the progress of the inner revolution. Each day took me further towards a paring-down of speech and action. Maybe I would just grind to a halt. Sarah and Jane grew more and more anxious and I shunned even their company. I had no visits, having long since told my visitors not to come to Durham. I knew what their reaction would be when they saw the wing. I went to church in the vain hope that God would recognize my desperation; but I should have known that He had crossed me off His list of people to extend His helping hand to.

There came a night where I was given a slightly different dosage of medicine – a little more. I swallowed it down and nodded to the nurse, who watched me guardedly.

I went back to the cell, where I felt the usual buzz. But then there was a different feeling, a feeling of losing hold of something . . . . I sat on the bed and rocked myself to and fro. I rocked, and I rocked, and I worked myself up to the pitch of longing and despair. Around my neck was the Walkman I had been half listening to. I saw a glass jar in my cupboard. We were allowed glass. I picked it up and flung it against the wall. It smashed and immediately I picked up the pieces, drawing the most jagged of them into my arms and hands. The first cuts brought some blood.

I had no sense of sanity. I scratched furiously with the glass and started on my legs, bare for night-time. They too yielded blood easily. I wanted something else. I picked up the Walkman and flung it across the room. It smashed against the wall too and lay, its contents spilling out on to the cold shiny floor. Blood dripped a little on to it.

I sawed again at my wrists. I looked around the cell. More glass. I flung that too. China, all the glass, anything that made a wholesome resounding crash went too. I dragged all the bedclothes off the bed and the clothes out of the little cupboard. I moved the glass frenziedly now, wanting to scratch out the pain.

Banging on the door. My heart sank. I sat still, twisted in the discarded bedclothes. The officer called to me. I didn't answer. She ran. Soon two men and another female officer came. The door was unlocked. I still sat mute. They tried to pull the glass away from me. I was not having that. I held on. The man was big and strong. He tugged and I gripped. His hand was sawn raw by the glass. Mine was already wet with blood. He yelped with pain. Still I hung grimly on. The other man prised my fingers away. Eventually I conceded the glass. The officer swore at me. The females stood rather helplessly. I would not look at them.

Somehow I was taken up to the strip cell. I was given a brown nylon dress to put on and handed some blankets made of similar stuff. The door was slammed to. I crouched in a corner and felt safe at last.

The cell was monk-bare. A single light bulb, protected from naughty fingers by thick perspex, hung red and warm. Two huge pipes flanked the window wall. I moved to them and sank down on to their comforting heat. The window itself was far too high for sight. Good. A bare grey mattress was the bed. An upturned cowboy hat sat in the corner of the room. Nothing else. I wondered where to pee. No taps.

I sat and rocked again, scratching my wounds. After a while, a doctor came in. He knelt and examined my hands and arms and legs. He peered at me, gently. He bandaged me and gave me some medicine to quieten me down. Then the door was locked again. I felt sleepy quickly but would not succumb. My hands stung. Tears squeezed themselves out of my sore eyes. I curled up by the pipes and thought . . . .

The next morning brought the repercussions it might be expected to. Psychiatrists wanted to know why. I saw no reason now why I should have to answer them. I was not accountable to them any longer. I thought that their reign of power was ended. They talked to me, and noted with frightening perception that I was depressed. They gave me drugs with no names and I took them happily. I had no reason not to now. I sat on the pipes, my place of safety, all morning and alternated between crying — still the dry, racking sobs — and staring into space, thinking about the past. The nurse came to ask me if I wanted a shower. I focussed on her with difficulty and declined. What for? I wasn't going anywhere. I thought this was funny. Another dose of medicine. I lay down and hugged the pipes. The day passed without my registering it. No one was allowed to see me in case they upset me. That was good. I didn't want anyone. I had my cuts and sore stinging body. I had my dreams and my tears. What else should I want? I was not allowed to get dressed in case I hanged myself with my shirt. I sat in the nylon dress and a dressing gown that looked moth-nibbled. The room was flooded with sunlight, dim through the frosted perspex window high in the wall.

The days and the nights blurred comfortingly into one. I lay close to the warm pipes and shivered only at the thought of having to leave that room. I felt safe there. I would not eat or drink, but eagerly took the medicine they gave me. I was tried on all different sorts until something was found which 'suited me'. Showering was a necessary and comforting daily agony: the cuts on my arms and legs stung and ached on contact with the hot water and soap. Pain seemed to be the only thing I could feel. I had no sense of humiliation as I sat and huddled all day in only my nightshirt and dressing gown.

I saw too many doctors and psychologists, who prodded and poked as far inside my psyche as they could, made mysterious notes on pieces of paper and then went away. My system went up and down yoyo-fashion with the constant and confusing changes of drugs. I lived for each dose. It blocked out all the near pain; this way I distanced myself to face only what I was able to at the time. I had a breathing space. I wept sometimes – for Alex, and for my mother, and for the tragedy of it all.

I developed a tactic which made perfect sense to me. After my slashings of that first frenzied night I had metaphorically licked my wounds, like a small, contented but deeply hurt animal, and had not thought any more of it. At eight o'clock at night the door would be closed and the last dose of medicine given out, and I would then be left alone to thrash in frustration. The hours would tick by and I would write and write, waiting for the time when the radio would croak back into action at four. I began to realize that part of my frustration was the lack of hardship that my brief interlude had brought me. The wounds had hurt for a while, but only a while, and they were not enough. I hunted around and soon found a tool.

The toothpaste tube, that container of all that is good and healthy, became a weapon for me to scratch and cut and hurt myself with. Nightly I dragged it sharply, rawly again and again over the wounds, still pink with recovering tissue. Nightly I felt the pull to do this until I could not let myself relax until I had done enough of it to know that in the morning I would be in agony. It became obsessive and precious. I felt again a small flame of contentment that I had found something to do that satisfied the self-destruct button in me. I had no idea that it was highly unhealthy, and was viewed with horror by civilized people. I felt better when I had done it, as I recorded in my diary.

> Well, it seems that at last I have found a kind of solution; I am actually capable of self-mutilation in one form or another. I have scarred arms and legs and wrists, yet not enough. Tomorrow I will be weighed and I must not eat or drink, except the medicine that I need with an obscene sort of craving.... I have been thinking about the appeal, hope it is not a retrial, more drawn-out pain... feeling a bit woozy now, but don't feel comfortable. Why the fuck should I? Guilt makes the bed hard. I was just thinking that I was getting better, and now I realize with what degree of distortion I see everything.
>
> Why am I frightened about the appeal when it is my own decision to go through with it? It is ridiculous.... Is it self-persecution, a wind-up, or just the vestiges of a last desperate hope? I think hope left me a long, long time ago. There goes! Good, I got more blood tonight, now I might let myself sleep.
>
> In the blood I see evil seeping out, slowly... there will be scars, I hope, to remind me and to bear witness to the pain.

All my confused thoughts at this time went down on those pages:

> 9a.m.... tense, very nervy. Sweaty palms... my pulse is racing like a mad thing.
> 12a.m.... saw the psychologist... is this helpful? Why do I need a psychologist?
> 1.30p.m.... talked a lot with Sister about childhood things. Feel easier but also feel and look knackered. Sis told me to lie down. What else do I do all day up here?
> 4.15p.m.... medicine time. Feel calmer as soon as I take it.

7p.m. . . . more medicine, different one again tonight, an old-fashioned one called Weldorm. Feel a bit sleepy.

8p.m. . . . locked in properly. Feeling dopey still.

9.10p.m. . . . beginning to feel wide awake.

10p.m. . . . still no effects.

11p.m. . . . now I'm getting pissed-off.

Midnight, ten past . . . writing to Mona. I'd like her to be there at the appeal. I don't want anyone else there, they will get all upset. Mona will understand that that's the way things are when it fails. My hair needs cutting, even though I can't see it I can feel it getting straggly. I look awful again today, I think it's all these different medicines.

1a.m. . . . *Why can't I just go to bloody sleep????*

4a.m. . . . *every time I look at my hands I look away. They are the root of all the evil, or is that too easy to say and turn my thoughts away from the evil that lies inside my head? They are the one incongruously lovely feature I have and they must go.*

5.20a.m. . . . I don't actually want to live but I'm too scared to die. I want to hurt again outside on my body where I can see a reason for the pain. Here goes.

7a.m. . . . unlock soon. I can hear the usual noises. My hands and breasts ache. Hope they don't find the metal and take it away from me.

8.30a.m. . . . unlock now. Shower time perhaps? Christ, it's going to hurt when I get under the shower with all these wounds.

9a.m. . . . Blood washed away again. Hurts like shit.

On the 13th:

One year since conviction . . . into the second year. Must remember when I go down to Holloway to take plenty of paper as I guess I'll be in a bad state.

Weighed again today . . . have lost, of course; as yet no appetite. Cannot sleep or relax, keep thinking only fifty days to go until the appeal hearing. I need to do something, wish for a razor blade. I've got to the stage now where I realize that I just don't care any more... for myself or my sanity or my health... I have felt now for months in the grip of a slow, scarring, dreadful pain that seeps in and out of me.

A few days later:
 5a.m. .... I want to die. I can cry – still no sound – but I don't want to wait any more for release of body. Yet I'm still too scared to die... isn't that strange?... I feel like my soul is crying out for tenderness and love, but without any hope of it... it's drying up like a waterless plant.

The following day:
 Today a strange thing is occurring. I am totally relaxed – not dopey, or sleepy, but relaxed and loose in mind and body. How long must it be since I have felt comfortable with myself? I have to try to drag myself back to the real world before the court hearing takes me by surprise.
 Of course – I'm on a much bigger dose today, that's what it is. I *do* feel a bit spacey.
 4a.m. .... I can feel all of it hang heavy on my mind, and there's that song on the radio, Otis Redding's 'Sittin' on the Dock of the Bay'. Makes me sad... I think a lot about Alan lately, and Alex, but can't stand those thoughts... I don't think of *her*, it hurts too much, although the pain is dulled the more I hurt my body with cuts and slashes. I think I need the pain – it is necessary to me, I breathe easier with it. Drifting in between it now... daydreams and a sort of insane unworldliness, I wish I could stay like this forever, not ever get dressed again or see people or do things that hurt except those that I choose... tonight I cannot sleep and yet I am having the biggest dose ever of Largactil. Why is this? Wide awake at four o'clock but wanting sleep. Too painful to lie down – my fault.

I can hear the chimes of the clock on the hill that I can't see.

Although I could not sleep, I felt no tiredness. Most of the day the door to my cell would be unlocked even though I rarely went out. Every day the Governor and his acolytes would come to peer at me, which was part of the morning procedure – all prisoners in special cells had to be seen by the Gov. He smiled vaguely at me, nodded, and asked me if I was all right. I would get the beginning of a sentence out and then be interrupted:
'Well, how are we today?'
'I'm – '
'Good, good. I'll be around tomorrow.'
He would then be carried away by his minions, eager to show him the latest security purchase.
Eventually the prison officers found my toothpaste tube, rusted and dirty, and, horrified, insisted that I had a tetanus injection in case the rust had got into my blood. I should be so lucky, I thought gloomily. It was not a suicide mission that I was on, as they seemed to think, but rather a slow, lingering tumult of pain. The staff did not always know if I had injured myself or not. I became crafty and took to scratching wounds only on my breasts and thighs, which could not be seen. Shower times became moments of dread anticipation. I came to recognize the perversity of what I was about, but could not stop the obsession. I even began to sleep a little when the cuts I had made were particularly painful. Self-destruction it might be, but by God it was easier to sleep at nights . . . .
The days went on like this, and I was a mass of festering wounds and sores. I still walked about in my nightshirt and dressing gown, which every now and then Sarah removed from me almost by force and washed. I saw myself in a mirror one day and was interested to find that I no longer cared how awful I looked. I received letters but did not reply. I often left them unread – they were always tainted for me by the knowledge that someone else had read them first. In my case, several people read them – not just the warders, but the nurses had to check, they

said, that there was no upsetting news in them which might make me worse. I often told them that the whole point was that there was nothing left to happen now – it had already taken place. That was why I had no cares about how I looked, about how far I went into the world which had become mine.

There came a time where the call of the Church nearly brought me to the brink. The priest there, a converted Catholic, the worst kind, tried all manner of subtle blackmail to get me back on to the path of righteousness from which I had strayed. I was amazed that he could be oblivious to my complete lack of interest in God at this time. He rode roughshod over the nurses' objections that he would upset the patient, and sneaked in past the chief nurse, a tiny, completely spherical figure whose squawks of protest could be heard every Wednesday as he ascended the stairs.

After what seemed to me a blissfully selfish reign of mine up there on the hospital, the nurses began to try to persuade me to get back into life on the wing. I was taken for trips back down to my cell, and whilst there I picked up large chunks of the broken glass which still lay on the floor. It had been left for me to clear up when I was well enough to be back on the wing proper – all part of the stringent punitive regime. Anyway, I would hardly have expected another inmate to clear up my blood and mess. I put the glass in the pocket of my dressing gown. I felt slightly sick that I had done so much damage, but it was only my own things. If it had not been I would have been in grave trouble.

Back upstairs, I was asked if I would like to put on my own clothes again. I did *not* like. I shrank from it. It seemed to me to be a step towards normality and I did not want that yet – if ever. I was scared of going downstairs, scared of the cold, cold cell. I liked it here, where I had the warm pipes and the comforting red light and the mattress on the floor and the cowboy hat. (I had discovered that this was the strip cell equivalent of a potty. It was cardboard and it leaked.

So they relented, and told me that if I was not ready

yet, I would have to see more psychiatrists. God help me, I thought wearily. More ... I had already seen ten by then. Wasn't that enough? But I complied – anything to stay where I was.

Of course, I had forgotten all about the appeal; I wanted to forget about it. I was as sure that it would be unsuccessful as I had been about the trial. It seemed to me to all be so irrelevant now. I didn't even want to be on the wing with the other women, have visits, face a court, let alone be thrust abruptly back into society. I dared not think about it all.

And then in February, thrusting me rather brutally back into thought and reality, two things happened. The first was the setting of the date for the appeal: it was to be 28 March. The other was an affidavit from Dr Dalton, the endocrinologist who had asked for a blood sample to be taken from me. I had quite forgotten her. It took a while for the words of the affidavit to penetrate because the language was very technical and I was still easily confused.

> Pre-menstrual syndrome is defined as the recurrence of symptoms before menstruation with complete absence of symptoms in the post-menstruum ... the normal levels of progesterone in healthy women who have no pre-menstrual syndrome are between 50-80nmols/1. A sample of Miss Reynolds' blood was taken and the level was found to be extremely low at 14nmol/1. The evidence I have obtained together with consultation with Miss Reynolds and the result of the test suggest that at the time of the offence Miss Reynolds was suffering from pre-menstrual syndrome and post-natal depression of sufficient severity to lead to temporary loss of control and this abnormality was such that it substantially impaired her mental responsibility for the killing.

Dr Dalton recommended immediate treatment with progesterone pessaries to correct the deficiency – legitimate enough for the authorities to accept now that it was in print. When I wasn't bleeding, I used them. The staff would only let me have one at a time in case I glued the locks up with the stuff, or ate them, or something strange like that.

The affidavit answered some questions for me in that, sceptical as I had been at the first mention of the PMS idea, I had to admit that for years I had felt strange around period time. The trouble was that, with so many valid reasons in my life for being and feeling strange, it was difficult to identify yet another. I was interested now to see if the progesterone made a difference. (It was the morning after the onset of the breakdown, the smashing up of my cell, that I had started to bleed.)

The fixing of the court date disturbed me more than I had expected. I was shaken and unnerved. It made everything that I had so far evaded, locked away inside myself in H Wing, rush to the fore. It brought the expectancy of failure and of anti-climax stinging back to me. I would be pulled out of my womb, made to present myself in court once again.

With the news of the date everyone on the wing began a concerted effort to restore me to normal. Sarah and the others came up the stairs to the hospital cell to see me, to try to talk me into getting dressed, eating, talking, thinking about the move to Holloway and the court. The nursing staff tried to persuade me to send out visiting orders to the family, to answer letters, to read the letters I received. But self-protectively I shrank into myself and would not succumb to their wheedlings.

One day I got hold of a pair of scissors and hacked my unruly hair into what I thought, mirrorless, to be a sort of a bob shape. Sarah put her hands to her mouth in horror when she saw me, and nearly cried. I did not care what I looked like: the uglier the better. Somehow the outside should resemble the raw, ugly bareness of the inner me. I felt cleansed, as if I had scraped the inside of my mind and body and was reborn. Not purged, or guiltless, but with a different, new, shaky, infant-like awareness of everything.

Grudgingly, I gave in to my own desire to walk around the tiny exercise yard with Sarah. The air was cold and fresh, and I was amazed that I had forgotten so quickly what it felt like. My legs were weak with lack of exercise and my eyes ran in the biting wind. I relished it all and let Sarah knit me some gloves and a huge, all-enveloping scarf to protect my already pink ears and nose from the weather.

And so I came back to life, as was inevitable, much as I wished my inertia would last forever. I had hibernated in the winter of my own despair, and had crept out a different creature. Energy came back to me, furious energy that left no room for compromise but spurred me to kick and flail, however uselessly, against the walls that held me. Life was mine again, and I set about slowly and determinedly trying to regain what I had lost – self-respect, self-love. Freedom? I don't remember ever consciously wanting that commodity, at least not in the physical sense. I was freer than I had been for a long time in the shadow of the chains I had broken myself.

But of course the path of my return to life was slower and more gradual than that. To those who had not seen me for a while, though, it was an alarming change. They were in two minds about my breakdown. One opinion was that it was a terrible, irreversible thing from which I would surely emerge a broken person; the other that, at least while I was passive, a 'victim' of prison, I was out of trouble, quiet, acquiescent, lifeless. I was also seen to be being punished by some unseen Fury. I read something when in H Wing composed by a former resident of the wing:

I don't know what to write . . . .

Not so long ago I cried when I saw a sunset over the cathedral, feeling insanely jealous of all things free.

Chain me to a wall, then. Give me bread and water, let me know what you really mean, for Christ's sake. Kill me.

You can never understand. I couldn't boil a kettle myself. I couldn't cross the road. Children would terrify me. And supposing someone ordinary should be polite to me? What would I do? I've forgotten.

I'm finished . . . and there is nothing I can do.

And in some ways, reading that, I felt that my newness, my childlike state in which I had nothing left, gave me the strength to try to forge something new from the ruin of the old life that had been almost wiped away those last few months. I felt as if I had aged immeasurably, and I felt a little wiser.

I saw Graham, my probation officer. He had seen the affidavit, and he said that he felt hopeful about the appeal. But I did not really want to think about that – I was not interested in such speculation. I mooched about the wing, and was soon made to return to work. It would be 'good for me to have something to do', they said, but added that in view of my gynae problems I was not to lift anything and not to scrub too much in case the bleeding got worse. However there were times when only Sarah and I worked on the wing, the others being in the workshop or with the doctor or somewhere like that, and in all fairness I could not let her do all the heavy work. The Sister would squeak with disapproval and trot down the stairs to tell me off whenever she caught me lifting.

But things had changed so much within me that I was prepared to set my own limits about what was too much. I was no longer prepared to have an officer walk over the newly, rawly scrubbed floors of my still embryonic self-respect. The days began with the familiar dread of monotony. Sarah saw the restless change in me and worried that I would start trying to kick against things. But I had no intention of wasting my precious and new-found energy on petty issues; I was saving it up.

I started to question everything, the rights and wrongs of each situation. I saw no point in the rules, so small and so cruel, which governed our lives to the nth degree. I questioned, and no answers came, because there were no answers. 'Because' was not good enough any more. I had outgrown the stage of passivity and I demanded some sort of logic or justification. These were not forthcoming either.

Things started to move once more. I was suddenly told that before the appeal I was going back to Holloway for legal visits. A strange feeling hung about the wing before my departure, a mixture of envy from those who had no appeal to hope for, and anxious hope from those who cared and who believed that the appeal should be a success. Sarah was red-eyed on the morning of my leaving. I told her that I would be back, and to keep baking cakes for my return. She shook her head, solemn, seeming to know something I did not. We did not hug – the moment too emotional for that; I did not want to start crying on the day I was going back to Holloway.

The women of the wing assembled to see me off, laden down with boxes and bags, followed by lots of officers. The women were silent, a waiting crowd. They called out messages of luck from the windows and Sarah cried. I felt a moist sadness inside me and swallowed it away.

Chapter Twelve

It took all day to drive back to London; I sat huddled up, dreading the moment of arriving and facing the inevitable questions I would as always encounter in the receptions area. I would know no one now; all my companions, those temporary saviours of my sanity, would have long since left. I felt cold and scared and insignificant, and the future seemed bleaker than ever before.

The date set for my hearing was a Friday. Friday did not seem to be my lucky day. At least it was not the 13th of the month.

I felt cold, always so cold. What was the matter with me? I was also defiant, inside my mind. I showed no outward signs of this defiance – I was not sure enough of my ground yet. I was angry, and I *felt*. It had been a long time since I had felt anything other than the dullness of monotony and despair, not even strong enough to produce rage. I had no idea where this new-found defiance should be directed.

The time at Holloway went intolerably slowly. I counted the days. I counted the hours. I could not believe how frustrating waiting could actually be. I had never waited for anything as indefinable as this. At the trial I had been fairly sure what was going to happen. Now I had no intuition, no feelings at all. Optimism was foolhardy and inappropriate, and pessimism was contradictory since it had been with my agreement that I had been sent for this last test. I knew that I would go through the same Hell that I had experienced during the trial, and two years' distance between the facts did not, could not lessen their power to horrify and sicken me.

I was stronger now, but weaker too. The breakdown had been so severe and damaging as to throw my whole existence into new and honest perspective. It had also made me far more vulnerable. I had not bargained for that. I had thought that I had already reached the lowest pitch of my vulnerability, but what I had not realized was the power of facing the truth about the inner self and how naked I had laid myself in the process. I did not yet know whether it had been worth it. The appeal would test me out again. This feeling like a child was a new experience for me – it had not happened when it should have done, or at any rate not for as many years as it should have done.

This time in Holloway I was sent to a wing that contained mainly long-term prisoners. I was not forced to work all day at first and so I was able to keep to myself as much as possible. I spent most of the days hiding in the cell, nervous of the large spaces of the wing after Durham's tiny confined landings.

I read most of the day, any old rubbish I could get my hands on to occupy my mind and prevent thought and speculation. In the course of it I came across some wonderful poetry:

> *I have lived many lives, and*
> *I have seen the city as one huge hospital*
> *Racked with disease, life itself*
> *An epidemic, raging out of control*
> *For which, in the end, there could*
> *Be only one cure.*
>
> *I have pondered these questions*
> *A thousand times, all the way back*
> *To my own peculiar outpost of despair*
> *And found no answer*

Fear came swiftly to me at this time. If the thing I dared not voice should happen, and in time it would have to anyway ('They can't keep you forever . . . . '), how would I find life? By now, two years on, almost, I was so accustomed to life in tones of grey and black that I almost welcomed the pain because it was now familiar and constant to me.

I was still on almost the same dosage of anti-depressant that I had had in H Wing. I did not like the residual effect of the drug, though, as I wrote in my diary: 'I don't like this feeling that the drug is controlling me rather than the other way around . . . also it makes me feel blank, sometimes, as if I have no feeling left, but it is an illusion because I know that I can feel again.'

The date for the dreaded day crept nearer and nearer. I felt more and more unavoidably pessimistic.

> Please God let it be over quickly. I can't bear the thought of a year's wait for a retrial . . . mornings are the worst . . . every day drags so endlessly. I even wish I were back in Durham where although I hate it I feel safer. There are no challenges and no responsibilities there, and I do not even have to think for myself. My life there is clearly defined into a pattern, as is every woman's there, and we either obey or risk even crueller confinement . . . a prison within a prison within a prison. There is no room for defiance or for freedom of thought or speech . . . even memories are locked up.

There was of course no room for defiance anywhere in the prison system, but I didn't think of that. I wanted to be heard, to reason with the nonsense that I heard paraded as rules, as reasons in themselves.

My visitors came with faithful regularity. I quite liked to see them now, but hated the anticipation that shone quietly on their hopeful faces. They dared not say to me what they felt in case, as before, they had all expected one thing and had to accept a vastly different other. I feigned optimism and no longer cried on these visits. I was tougher, a little harder, the naïvety and the surprise gone from me. I was no longer eighteen years old and stupid enough to be hoping for anything.

Things were hard and alien for me at Holloway now. Women who did not know me, but saw from the card above my cell door that I was a lifer and nineteen years old, wondered what I had done with a morbid and thirsty curiosity that they had to satisfy. What else was there to fill their time but gossip of such a dreary and sickening nature? I could no longer even attempt explanations, and in my new-found and ill-fitting guise of quiet defiance saw no bloody reason why I should parade the frontiers of my pain simply for their pleasure. I refused to tell, to talk about H Wing – another item of interest because of its well-deserved notoriety. I was not popular in a world where talk and revelations were all.

I was told after a while that I was required to do something with my days. They wanted me to work. This was fine. I too wanted to work, to occupy my days, to fill my mind with mindless rubbish, to worry not about my perilous future and my ruined life but about how clean the floors were and if there was a scrap of dust to be seen on the shelves in the officers' office. But this was not exactly what they had in mind.

Instead I had a brief spell working with some dignity in the education department as an assistant to the cookery teacher, and was then told that I was to move from the long-term-sentenced wing where I was beginning, shakily, to find my feet and get along with the women, to the wing considered to be the worst. It was full of the troublemakers whom no one knew how to deal with. It was thought that by having them all on one wing together, and staffing that wing with the strictest officers, the trouble could be contained within that one area. My blood ran cold at the idea, but the reality was even worse. The noise was constant and unrelenting. Screaming and shouting and raging arguments went on from morning until night. Women who had been all around the system and ended up there were, unsurprisingly, pissed off. So, for once, was I.

In the days immediately before and just after the appeal hearing I confided my thoughts to my diary:

22 March 1988

    I guess I'm feeling so odd because of the court date so near. Every second seems, I swear it, to be exploding into hours. I am getting very unnecessarily angry at small things, like not getting to see the doctor when I need my medicine. No sleep tonight, then.

23 March
I think I ought to stop trying to presuppose events... I feel totally shattered with the effort of thought and worry. At least I can, I guess, let off a little extraneous steam tomorrow when I see poor Graham. He should be glad he's on holiday while the hearing is on. I'm quite sure he wouldn't want a repeat of last year's fiasco with weeping women on his hands. However he's a real support to me and I will try not to pile my mental shit on to him.

24 March
God... can't imagine how to deal with Monday. I should expect to be tense, irritable, etc. That dark, hopeless depression has abated a little to be replaced by an almost unbearable tension. I really must have some Valium.
8.15p.m. Thank *God* for Valium. My request is the doctor's desire. He must know that I am officially beyond salvation. He has been told to grant my every request. Oh goody!

27 March
It's ridiculous. Here I am sitting in my cell cross-legged and I read in an out-of-date paper that *Out of Court* and *Rough Justice* are filming about me at the moment for use after the hearing if it goes unsuccessfully. Now I wish someone could tell me – who defines success.
3a.m. No sleep of course. Ha!! I'll be shouted at in three hours to get up. I *am* up... and dressed.

28 March
9.30p.m. Well.... I'm back at Holloway. Home. I'm absolutely knackered. What is it, I'd like to know, about a court room that wears you out? It's not exactly as if you are allowed to go running all

over the place exploring your environment. The cells there were so small we practically had to sit on each other's knees.

It's over, I suppose, except for the little matter of the final verdict, I mean. I did actually feel very . . . secure, I think is the word, at the court. With all the security there I couldn't really feel otherwise. It wasn't for me or anything, it's just the way that they are there.

I have to see another psychiatrist. I've done a count – in just under two years I've seen fourteen different ones. Given the choice I would have seen only one or two of those. And anyway, what difference will one more make? It will almost certainly be a man, another man, disapproving, judgemental, to slot neatly into the man's, man's, man's, man's world of the courts. It's true – all the lawyers and the judges, the doctors, the solicitors, the witnesses, are all men. Oh – of course, the secretaries and clerks and messengers are women. But they're kind of incidental, intentionally I think.

I'm sleepy now, due to the sweet drug of peace I've just imbibed. God, how quickly I lapse into dependency. Once again . . . . And why not?

29 March
Woke up this morning thinking I had to go back to court again today. Wishful thinking, that.

The previous day, much had gone on at court. We had first of all ended up at the wrong place. The screws thought we were going to the CCC, which is the Old Bailey. We were of course supposed to be at the CCA, the Appeal Court. A or C here or there makes a lot of difference, you know.

When we eventually did arrive, we had to get up six flights of stairs with eight boxes, most of them carried by me – they were mine, it is true, but do I have eight pairs of arms? There is this unwritten rule that the inmate carries her own stuff and the screws dared not help. Blimey, I thought, breathless and bruised as we bumped up and down, up and down, times six, crocodile-style, is there a doctor in the court?

As it turned out, there were rather too many doctors in the court. In fact, everyone had turned up despite my efforts in February to get Roy to deny all knowledge of the date so that no one would be there. They had wormed it out of him and there they all sat, in best bib and tuckers, beaming hope at me over the sea of journalists and lawyers.

The Appeal Court was far more practical than the Crown Court had been. I no longer had the press at my elbow, able to observe every sigh, to hear every whisper, to capture every expression. They were tucked away almost out of sight. The judges, three of them, were in a row alongside me, at the same level as me. There were microphones in front of each of them, and in front of me. How clever, I thought admiringly. Now if one of them is deaf or near mute, the microphone will amplify his words for us.

Remarkably, though, the judges were not senile, nor in their dotage. One looked as young as forty. The other two were older, but looked to be in full possession of their faculties. Well, I thought, things do seem to be looking up.

I don't remember all that much of the hearing because most of it was composed of the legal trivialities which had in fact enabled us to get this far – grounds of appeal, based on significant remarks made by the prosecution QC and the trial judge which were brought up, pored over and argued about. This seemed to take up most of the morning.

After a foodless lunch (I was uninspired by the mound of unidentifiable matter that lay slumped upon a plate) the court resumed. The lawyers' faces were a little redder than before, from which I deduced that they had fared better than I. The afternoon was no better than the morning. The main point of argument was the claim by the prosecution silk, Barker, that before the trial I had only been in custody for three days and so he had not had time to get a second, independent, doctor to see me. He claimed that my lawyers had prevented access to me at that time by the prosecution. In fact, at that moment he put his professional head into the noose.

I had been in custody for three and a half months before bail at a custodial hospital that my lawyers had no control over; it was only a week or so before the trial that he had requested that a second doctor should see me. I had then been available to the prosecution for eight months. My lawyers had suggested to him that at that stage it was too late for a second opinion to be productive, and that I had by then seen enough doctors. The reason for the request was because the original prosecution psychiatrist, Dr O'Connor, had by then submitted his report which was overwhelmingly favourable to the defence.

It was eventually agreed that Dr Dalton could give her evidence. It was also agreed somewhat wearily by the three judges, who seemed not to be enamoured of the pedantic and almost desperately stalling lawyer, that I could be seen by yet another doctor to settle the psychiatrist matter once and for all. I was not told who it would be, but visualized Barker scouring the country for a doctor who (a) disliked women, (b) disliked those convicted of any offence, and (c) would, hopefully, take a dislike to me. I even heard what I guess was just a rumour that he was trying to bring over some eminent American doctor who would cast a shadow on Dr Dalton's evidence.

The judges cast kindly looks at me, and one even winked, I thought. And I was right, I was not seeing things: the screw sitting next to me had seen the wink too. He stared at me intently and I felt empathy emanating from him. One of the judges, the most succinct one of the lot, seemed to be playing delicately with Barker the prosecutor, spinning him out almost indulgently on the line and then hauling it in again. They seemed to me to be giving him time, knowing that he would have to succumb in the end. But this was all supposition on my part, born of some very vague and intangible feeling.

By now the campaigners had appeared — all of them it seemed, for the court was certainly full. They had given themselves a moment of real fear. The most senior of the judges had announced in frosty tones that one of his colleagues had been in Brackley and had happened to ask one of the local people what the posters proclaiming 'Justice for Anna' were all about. He felt himself to be slightly compromised and had wondered whether or not to sit on the case. Everyone held their breath. But he had decided that he would. Silent sighs of relief. All three judges seemed to be very genuinely concerned for the defendant. I was amazed.

The hearing had ended with the judges smiling and bowing to Mr Barker's demands for yet another psychiatric report. So back to Holloway we travelled, armed with the promise of a very quick second court date. It was raining and the Strand looked glamorous to me with everyone confidently striding their way along the shiny pavements – crowds of people whose lives were in control. Whenever we drew up at the myriad traffic lights going out of the West End, cars alongside us stared, fascinated, at the caged animal. I looked back at them, searching their faces for the reactions.

On the wing, the next day, I hoped and waited for the news that I would go back to H Wing in the interim. No chance. I was informed that I had to work – I and several other women were to scrub the whole length of the trolley route which ran all around the inside of the prison, indoors and outdoors. It was undoubtedly the most frustrating job in the whole nick because every time part of the route was clean, the trolleys carrying one meal or another would rattle along and undo all the good work.

I knew straightaway that a job like that would wreak havoc with my poor womb and decided that I was not going to risk having a haemorrhage just when it was all presumably starting to heal after the harshness of the work in Durham. I decided that I would have to refuse to do the job. But it wasn't quite as simple and logical as that to the authorities. The officer in charge of the wing told me that I would go down to the punishment block if I refused the job, on whatever grounds.

I was lucky for a while. Reprieve came with the news that my job-to-be was postponed because the bad weather delayed the process. The task also involved carrying all the huge rubbish bins from one part of the prison to another. But of course the bad weather could not last forever, unfortunately for me. I wished, hoped, prayed even for rain, sleet, snow, to hold off the confrontation. Anything to avoid the moment of truth.

One morning the day began with a clear and blue sky. At 8a.m. the officer came and told me to go to work. I told her my reasons for refusing and explained that I would not, could not do it. A change came over her, from anonymously saccharine-friendly to tight-lipped anticipatory. I was then asked by the senior officer why I would not go to work. I explained again. I had just got to the part about the medical staff in H Wing being worried about my bleeding when she cut me short.

'Are you or are you not going to go to work?'
'No.'
'I am ordering you to go to work.'
'I'm sorry, but I'm not going to go. I can't.'
'I am giving you a direct order to go to work.'
'I'm not going. I just said so!'
'So you're refusing a direct order?'

Finally she's grasped the situation, I thought. She wasn't the most perceptive officer I'd ever met.

'Yes.'

Next thing, I was marched back to the cell by the silent officer and locked back in. A few hours later the door was opened and five officers, big girls all, marched in and stood, arms folded, by the door. One told me curtly to pack all my things and go with them. A moment of fear briefly sidled into my mind, and was gone.

An hour and three broken, split brown bags later we were on the block. I was strip-searched, body-searched, and my possessions thrown into the cell after me. The door was slammed to, and I was left alone.

I sat for a while in a daze and then got up to explore my surroundings. A bed, iron, with dirty mattress, graffiti'd pillow and shit-smeared wall. The cell held a source of company for me in my confinement – three cockroaches. They were very large and very black. I swallowed. This I was not sure about. I had not bargained that I would be encouraged, nay pressed, into keeping so many pets. The cell was not big enough for all four of us. Drowning seemed to be the kindest answer. The taps were stiff and, when pressed, yielded two more roaches instead of water. I began to wonder then if it might not have been more pleasant to have done the scrubbing and bled to death.

An hour later I had, I thought optimistically, seen the last of the creatures. They had, albeit with much frantic crawling up the sides of the thankfully slippery basin, disappeared down the plughole. Or so I thought. I discovered that they could crawl back up the plughole whenever they felt the need for a breath of air.

I was allowed to keep my books and Walkman and writing paper, and was content that first evening to sit cross-legged on the iron bed reading and trying to do yoga. I felt enormously relaxed compared with how I had been on the wing. I waited with some trepidation for the morrow, when I would have to go before the Governor or deputy to answer for my sins.

I slept uneasily, as always, the sleeping medicine working for a few hours, then my ever-present worry surfacing. I had nightmares almost every night – and worried about them, too, if they did not appear. The next day I was nervous, a little scared maybe. I was not a rule-breaker and I felt the edge of humiliation in me at being placed in the punishment block for trying to save my health.

The Governor was not present. One of his lackeys was, a thin, manlike woman who barked rather than spoke and issued orders as if to a little dog. The adjudication began. I was to stand facing the deputy, with two officers by my side facing me, backs to the deputy. This was presumably because I was slightly more easy on the eye than She Who Must Be Obeyed. I was asked why I had refused to work. I gave the same, now slightly rehearsed-sounding, answer as before, at which I was told that we would adjourn to have my story checked out and would reconvene in three days. In the meantime I would stay down on A1. Well, that's time for a thorough investigation, I thought hopefully. Three days is long enough to have the Yard in. Justice will be done!

I floated back to my cell and sat down. Bliss. No noise at all, no stomach-tightening demands from officers, no contact with nosey and pain-inducing inmates. I read three chapters that day and slept for eight hours that night. And this I had been afraid of . . . .

It did get a little worse, though. When the deputy resumed the report she informed me that the prison doctor's word was good enough for her. I told her that if she would get in touch with H Wing medical, they would put the matter right. She refused to do this. I knew also that my medical records had not come down from Durham with me, so no one had the authority to check whether or not I had or had ever had a gynaecological condition.

I was given three days' confinement to my cell and loss of all privileges. My mattress and bedding and pillow were removed by the officer, but the books and pens and paper stayed – they must be rights, not privileges, I thought. I sat on the iron bed and wondered why bedclothes were considered to be a privilege. I was informed by the self-righteous officer at the hatch that the object of this was to stop people on punishment sleeping or sitting in the daytime. At night I would get the bedding and mattress back, she said.

'So what am I supposed to do – stand all day?'

I was not cheeky, just curious to know if this was the idea.

'Not my problem.'

I made a makeshift seat with a bundle of clothes and my chunky dressing gown and sat on that. At midday I had my sedative and felt immediately sleepy. I was still on quite a large dose. Having no option, I curled up on the bare iron bed and fell asleep immediately. The price, of course, was terrible backache.

The officer was amazed. 'You're not supposed to sleep during the day. That's the whole point of taking the bedding away,' she pointed out.

'I know, but what can I do? Once I've had the midday dose, I'm out straightaway. What are you going to do, give me a bed of nails to make really sure I don't nod off?' I argued not unreasonably. After all, what else was there to do? I had all evening to read and write and stare out of the window and think and spin out ten minutes on a cup of tepid tea.

Something strange seemed to be happening to me. The doses of medicine I had three times a day were growing in quantity. This is what solitary confinement does to you, I thought at first. I'm seeing things. But I asked the nurse who brought the stuff, and for once got a straight answer. (Typically the doctor would write you up for 'something' but not tell you what it was. Then you would say to the nurse who brought it to you, 'What is it, please?' And she would say, 'It doesn't matter what it is. Do you want it or don't you?' And you would say, 'Yes, but I want to know what it is.' She would then tell you, angrily, to book the doctor and ask him what it was. You would then insist, 'But I don't want to see the doctor, I just want to know what it is.' This would go on and on and on.)

The dose had, in fact, nearly doubled. The little pots the stuff had come to me in originally had been replaced by a mug-size pot. Alarmed, I wanted to ask the doctor about this, but then I figured that they would take it away if I drew attention to it.

The three days of punishment continued, passed too quickly, and the badness in my stomach returned with the prospect of going back on to that horrible wing, and having to keep refusing to do the job. I was reassured by the punishment cell – albeit cockroach-ridden, iron-bedded, freezing cold and lonely – it was at least a safe place for me. I was always aware that if I let the dispensers of punishment know that I craved time down there they would switch to something else, deprive me of some privilege or other – although one thing they could not do was take away my visits from people outside, since visits are a right, not a privilege. It was a pretty hopeless situation. This desire to take away what is precious was not always from cruelty but often from a vague notion that to be any use prison is meant to be unpleasant, and that to give in to anything that caused pleasure might cancel out the sobering effect of the sentence.

So back to the wing I went, trailing my brown bags along the floor with a s-s-s-s-s- sound. That became my trademark. 'Oh, here's Anna again, back from/going to the block.' Once on the wing, I was immediately asked/told/screamed at to go to work. Once again I refused and we went through the whole procedure about was I refusing a direct order, and so on. Back in the cell, wait for the Heavy Mob. Brown bags and me down to the punishment cell. Next day, flanked by the Terrible Twins, facing the deputy. Same questions, same answers. After all, what had changed? By now I gritted my teeth and just pleaded guilty to the charge. It seemed sensible to do so since what I wanted was the punishment they would inevitably give me. This time, to my horror, they simply removed all my privileges and earnings (as a fine – God help them, were the prison finances in such a state of collapse that they really needed my £1.37 weekly 'wage'?) and sped me back up to the wing. The process repeated itself until I was given a long enough time on A1 to make it really worth while packing my bags.

I don't even know how I managed to spend all day doing not much of anything, but I must have done. Because there was nothing except thought, and the few books that I had – Dickens and Hardy and occasionally a library book, some trashy romance to while away a few hours without having to use my brain – and writing. I put down thoughts and feelings and fears and worries and tried to write out my pains. Sometimes it even worked. I sat in the heat of the sun – such as came through the window that was glazed with dull white perspex so you could only see through the slits – and watched troops of women go by to and from the education block, and wet-haired, with towels around their necks, from the gym and pool. I recalled lots of memories in my time down there being punished, some of them sweet and nostalgic, though when others came I had to change the track of my thoughts swiftly and self-protectively. But at least I could feel again – after the adoption I had thought that I was dead, emotionally anyway, and I had wished that I was. Now, I felt different. I couldn't say with total honesty that I wanted to die. I wanted something to change, I was trying to make it change, something big and painful and awkward in me, although I didn't know what it was exactly.

Mona had been released a short time before, and she came up to see me. She was shocked when she heard where I was, what wing I was on. 'That's not like you,' she said, dismay and puzzlement in her voice.

'I know,' I confessed. 'But I just had to stand up to it

for once – not to anyone in particular, but to the whole thing. It was too stupid to do the work and then be ill and blame myself for not having enough guts to take on the whole lot.'

She understood.

I was frustrated when trying to explain the same thing to my other visitors, Alan's mother, my relatives, because they lived in a different world, and they were not sure about my turning in one fell swoop from acquiescent and demure to antagonistic and demanding. But I, on the other hand, could no longer pretend that I was simply someone to please and pacify as I had been when I was younger. I had grasped the idea that I had to come to terms with myself and must respect the new me. Otherwise how could I expect anyone else to respect me?

I didn't always feel so sure that the 'child' I was creating inside me would turn out able to live in the world. I was teaching myself how to live all over again, and trying this time to get it as near right as possible. Sometimes it didn't even make sense to me either. I knew only that I had come to a turning point in my life and that this time there was only one choice. I could go out kicking and fighting, trying and probably failing, attempting to understand it all and to improve it. Or I could just let go of all of it, and let the backward slide begin. And there was only one way for that to end.

One of the sources of guilt in my mind was the fact that I rarely if ever answered letters. One correspondent (the reason for all these strangers writing to me was largely because a priest in Oxfordshire had asked his congregation to do so to buck my spirits up) wrote more and more often, eventually up to four times a day – I received letters, cards, even parcels and flowers. I was amazed at this.

As the days crept slowly by, never before had each minute seemed to be filled with so many extraneous seconds. I was worn out daily with the exhaustion of waiting, churning thoughts round in my brain and drawing no conclusions whatsoever. I spent my time still between the block and the wing, which I hated as much as ever. The women were so noisy, so nosey, and so bloody loud in everything they did, it seemed to me. But it didn't take much to irritate me then, waiting like that for the final court appearance to be over.

At last, with no warning, who should come to see me but the doctor sent by the prosecution. I felt he was just another of those shrinks who asked the same painful questions and interpreted silence suspiciously, and then went away having made their notes, leaving me to pick up the pieces of freshly roused grief and pain. Nothing new.

Although he was not a man given to pleasantries, he was not actually unpleasant, and I felt that this would, after all, be the last of these sessions of recall and memory and game playing that so exhausted me. He came in the afternoon, about four, and stayed until seven; I could feel dark circles appearing under my eyes. He was brisk, sharp even, to make me think and remember and talk, and I was sparing in my words, careful of my own shakily constructed defences. He saw that and did not push too hard. He had all the reports made previously on me, and had talked to other people such as Graham and the lawyers. There was not much more that I could tell him. He left, saying that he would return. I nodded, exhausted, and crawled back into the punishment cell. I lay on the mattress-less bed and cried, too tired and weak to make any noise.

When he came back, I had lost all track of the passage of time. I had no clock, no calendar, no sense of time except the vague regularity of mealtimes to guide me. I saw him and felt nothing but a dullness and a hope that he would not stir the unquiet grave I had made of my memories. He asked me only about my feelings concerning the appeal, about what could happen, and how I thought I would cope with life outside – all those kinds of questions. He put them in a rapid volley demanding answers which I, stupefied by the idea and possibility of the 'outside' coming nearer, could not give. Before he went he told me that he thought I would not be able to cope with life outside but that I should be given help and a chance to try to make it. I was immediately terrified. He tore a page out of his notebook and wrote upon it the name, address and telephone number of a psychiatrist who worked in the area where I had come from. I did not actually realize what he was doing this for.

Sometimes I did not know whether I wanted to be released or not, and turned the idea round in my head. I had forgotten, consciously perhaps, as part of my survival kit, what the words and the feeling would be like. Smells, sound, the streets, traffic – crossing the road! – men, those alien creatures. Babies in the street. Women who from the back or the side might look fleetingly like my mother, or men who might look like Alan. Girls with college degrees and unclouded eyes. And what would I do? Where would I go? What about jobs and things? It made my brain ache, so I stopped thinking about it.

I was lucky really, in some ways. The drugs I still took blanked out a lot of those worries. And, after all, it didn't take much. Just thoughts about H Wing, and long years there stretching ahead of me, were enough to convince me that thoughts of outside were groundless fears. I was grateful for the undemanding blankness of my days.

And then the date for the last day at court came: 22 April. I was alerted only a week or so beforehand, as were the lawyers and all the supporters. They would all be there, they said. But I did not want anyone there. I wanted to experience by myself what I saw as an inevitable anti-climax. The night before I wrote in my diary:

> Last day on the block. God, I can't stop thinking about tomorrow. I hope that no one is there, but I know that they will all be. I suppose I can't bear the thought of a repeat performance of the trial.
>
> **4a.m.** Why can't I sleep tonight? Guess! God, I hate this cell. Vomit and shit – the smells get trapped from the previous occupants. Yuk.

The morning came eventually. I felt blank-eyed and wretched with wakefulness. Leaving the cell, I felt a moment's strange affection for it. It was my safety, and today was yet another day of uncertainty. Dragging my stuff in the perennial brown bags down to receptions and out to the van, I wondered if it would be the last time.

I had sat amid the utter chaos of the morning receptions rush hour and watched everyone get ready for their court dates.

On the way, I sat silently anticipating events for my own benefit. The day will go quickly, I thought. And when it is over, the press will go quickly too, to their telephones and offices. The judges and the clerks will have left already, as soon as it is over. Like an execution. I will feel the stale taste of anti-climax heavy in my mouth and I will be knackered by the end of the day. A graffiti-strewn bed in a shit-smeared cell crawling with cockroaches will await me. So, you see, nothing will change.

But I must not presuppose, today. I will sit, and wait, and wait, and wait . . . eventually I move with the officers into the same court room as last time. I do not feel too alien here. The judges regard me with some interest. To them I am just another creature, perhaps pathetic, perhaps evil, who passes through their day. They do not even reflect on how their decision today will shape my life.

I am writing in the present tense because it is as clear and bright in my head and on my tongue as if I were there again, even more than eighteen months later.

The room is quiet. The judges file in and we all sit. They are fine-looking, with noble, faintly aristocratic profiles.

The talk is very technical. It is of the PMT test, and the findings of the last psychiatrist. The doctor gives his views and the judges nod sagely. They understand a little of what he says. I do not, mostly. This is a privilege of class. Maybe.

I want to stretch, to yawn, to stand up and walk about. Once again I am fairly detached. It is all taking too long.

The judge is saying something to me. I do not focus on him quickly enough to catch his words. I nod to look as if I have been listening. Everyone looks happy. They are all smiling. I feel like a child, irrationally – left out of the joke, too slow to catch on. I want to cry.

Led down the stairs at the lunch recess, I am sweating. I refuse even the cup of tea brewed by the male officers who run the court below stairs.

I need my midday dose of drugs. I can feel myself getting nervous, paranoid. The insistent, sickening need creeps over me.

Back into court. Everyone still smiling. The senior judge is smiling too, talking to me. He leans forward and I see the layers of tiny lines around his eyes. He is telling me that he wonders whether a short prison sentence might be good, to exorcise my need for punishment. He says that on reflection he has considered the opinions of the doctor and probation officer and feels that probation would be the best thing. I sit unbelieving, unaware that the verdict has been changed.

A woman is now standing up. She looks a little wild, a little strange. I do not know who she is. She is saying that she will take psychiatric responsibility for me. My probation officer makes a similar promise of responsibility and supervision when I am released. Released?

The judge is turning to me again. The officer next to me hisses to me that I am to stand up. I am weak-kneed suddenly. The judge tells me that he is going to release me on a two-year probation order, and asks if I know what that entails. I nod, dazed. Does it matter? He seems to think so. He has a twinkle in his eye, I am sure. Alan's mother, Pat, appears in the box to tell me that she will give me a home for as long as is necessary. Everyone is smiling again. The press are itching to escape and find a phone. After an eternity, I am told to get down from the dock and am escorted by the now silent and strangely unfriendly officer down the stairs to the cell area.

I am a little worried. I thought they said release. Why the cells? Panic rises in me. Is it all a joke? Why am I back down here? I do not understand. My enquiries are met with blankness. The atmosphere has changed, subtly. As a prisoner I am accepted, pitied even, cooed over. As a free woman, am I someone to be feared, that the heat of revenge for treatment issued may be turned upon them? It is all too ridiculous.

I am asked to sign forms releasing me and my property. I am given a green form which they tell me is for the DHSS, and £26 which is to keep me, surely, in the style to which I have become accustomed. I am shown to my various brown bags and cardboard boxes and told to get on with it. No goodbyes are issued, or wishes of good luck, or even smiles. They are now frozen, not a part of my life any more. I realize, and back away without a word.

Eventually all my belongings are stowed in a taxi, by other hands. I am told to stay round the back of the court, for there are a few press people outside. I sigh, weary suddenly. Mona comes forward and we hug, silently reaffirming a friendship which will be different now. Everyone else is tearful, hugging and kissing. I am aching for my own company.

I am told to sneak out the back way and jump into the taxi. But it seems to me that by doing so I will only bring the press crawling around some other way. I know these things. I tell them, all these people around me, that I want to go out the front way and walk away without shame. They are anxious, but know I won't change my mind.

I am not alone, as I would have wished to be, used to facing things with only myself and bravado for company. I walk out through the beautiful ancient arches of the building which has seen so many triumphs and so many tragedies, and is still standing, and that gives me the little courage I need to do this one last thing, to affirm in print, and on photographic memory, that I am ready, now, at last, reluctantly, fearfully but assuredly, to face whatever there may be out there. I do not yet know what it will be. It may be worse.

I see nothing for a moment except flashes of hot, white light, flashbulbs wildly trying to catch my expression as I walk down the steps. I shake my arms free of those who hold me for comfort, for I do not need it now. Journalists grab at me and shout and call my name, but it doesn't matter. It does not shake me. I know that this is it. I take a deep breath and shudder as I stand on the steps that are the remnant of all things captive, and I wait for a moment, my mind blank, with fear and nervousness and something else – excitement, hovering at the edges of my senses. For now, that will have to be enough. I walk forward, into the light of the day.

Epilogue

Of course, the absurd melodrama soon wore off. I was taken by friends to a house just off Baker Street, where I sat dazed, holding a mug of tea, while they watched themselves and me on the six o'clock news.

Now it is October 1989, over eighteen months since that strange day of official release. The past year and a half have been full of immense changes, ones that would not be extraordinary or enormous to most people but are so to me because they represent what I have not been used to: normality. I have come, not easily, to a sort of peace within myself most of the time – if I don't think too deeply, or examine my thoughts or dreams. I work, I live and I have friends, good friends; I have a lover, who is not perfect and thus accepts my imperfection.

It seemed a huge contrast to me at the time, between the freedom I have given myself – that of release from the bonds of life-threatening guilt and pain – and the freedom that the court granted me, the freedom to live without restraint. Almost from the day I was born I had been in prison, a prison mostly of my own making, one of tortuous indecision, of self-hatred, of guilt and of fear – fear of the God I was taught to fear, and fear of life itself. Freedom seemed almost too late for me, and yet I welcomed and embraced it, felt the sun hot on my skin, and the rain – rain! I had forgotten! And I went into shops and marvelled at their range and to my eyes beautiful array of goods, all colours, all choices . . . .

People amazed me too, and I caught my breath as I saw a woman who looked . . . well, I don't need to say, do I? I realized that that is something that will never lose its pain for me.

I felt as if I had been inside somewhere sheltered for ever, not simply two years. Everything seemed to have its own peculiar resonance and meaning, its own beauty, and that has not changed over my eighteen months of life in the real world.